Happy travels!

Laura Zahn

Room at the Inn/Wisconsin -

Guide to Wisconsin's Historic B&Bs and Country Inns

Laura Zahn

Down to Earth Publications
St. Paul, Minnesota

Published by **Down to Earth Publications**
1426 Sheldon
St. Paul, MN 55108

Copyright ©1987 by Laura Claire Zahn

All rights reserved. No part of this book may be reproduced or transmitted in any form or by any means, electronic or mechanical, including photocopying, recording or by any information storage and retrieval system, without the written permission of the author, except for the inclusion of brief quotations in a review.

First printing, October 1987

Library of Congress Cataloging in Publication Data.
Zahn, Laura Claire
        Room at the Inn/Wisconsin --
        Guide to Wisconsin's Historic B&Bs and Country Inns

1. Bed and Breakfast Accommodations - Middle West - Directories
TX 907.Z33   87-71414

ISBN 0-939301-02-4 (softcover)

Maps by Jim Miller

Photos by Laura Zahn

Pictured on the cover (and art provided by):
    Upper Left Corner - Thorp House Inn, Fish Creek
    Upper Right Corner - Chippewa Lodge B&B, Lac du Flambeau
    Lower Right Corner - the tower house at Bonnie Oaks Estate, Portage
    Lower Left Corner - The Old Rittenhouse Inn, Bayfield

To
Bill Karich,
gone but not forgotten

When I began this book, I expected to go out, see some nice places, hear some interesting stories, and learn a good deal. I knew full well that each inn and each innkeeper were stories in themselves.

What I *didn't* expect was that somewhere during late night talks or over breakfast with innkeepers, the line between interviewer and interviewee(s) was crossed. We became friends. And I felt the full weight of telling the stories of wonderful people and their special places. I hope I have done them justice.

Some folks not only shared their homes with me, but a part of their lives. Sometimes that has made the goodbye walk to the car an awfully long one, but it's also made this project a joy. Especially Ann and Buddy, Betha and John, Bill S., Chris and Sverre, Darlene and Tom, Joan S., Kathleen and Mike, Keith, Mary Jo and John, Patty and Jerry, Rosanne, Sharon and Wally -- you have made me a wealthy woman, regardless of the outcome of this enterprise!

To my readers: I now feel that wherever I go in Wisconsin, I am not far away from a friend. I hope that after you read this book and visit these places, you will feel that way, too.

What would I have done without Jim Miller, love of my life, partner in life, and a darned good map-maker, to boot? Or Kathy O'Neill, Ronda Allen (Wisconsin Division of Tourism), Maxine Jeffris, Mary and Ed Zahn or Karen Anderson (Special Places, Inc.)? Many, many thanks.

Table of Contents
Arranged by Wisconsin's Tourism Divisions & Door County

Preface & Introduction......*About using this guide*....... **11-19**

Map..............*Locations of all facilities in Wisconsin*.............. **20-21**

-Indian Head Country - North 22-47
- Area Map.. 22-23
- Cooper Hill House - Bayfield.. 24-25
- Greunke's Inn - Bayfield... 26-27
- Grey Oak Guest House - Bayfield... 28-29
- Le Chateau Boutin - Bayfield.. 30-31
- Old Rittenhouse Inn - Bayfield.. 32-33
- Pinehurst Inn - Bayfield... 34-35
- Woods Manor B&B - LaPointe (Madeline Island)...................... 36-37
- Seven Pines Lodge - Lewis... 38-39
- The Mustard Seed - Hayward.. 40-41
- The Stout Trout B&B - Springbrook...................................... 42-43
- The Willson House - Chippewa Falls...................................... 44-45
- Son-ne-Vale Farm B&B - Colfax... 46-47

-Indian Head Country - Rivertowns 48-61
- Area Map.. 48-49
- St. Croix River Inn - Osceola... 50-51
- Jefferson-Day House - Hudson.. 52-53
- The Yankee Bugler - Prescott... 54-55
- Great River Farm - Stockholm... 56-57
- Gallery House - Alma... 58-59
- The Laue House - Alma.. 60-61

-Northwoods 62-73
- Area Map.. 62-63
- The Inn - Montreal.. 64-65
- Chippewa Lodge B&B - Lac du Flambeau................................. 66-67
- Cranberry Hill B&B Inn - Rhinelander................................... 68-69
- Glacier Wilderness B&B - Elton... 70-71
- Lauerman Guest House Inn - Marinette.................................. 72-73

-Central Wisconsin River Country 74-93
Area Map 74-75
By the Okeag Guest House - Columbus 76-77
Bonnie Oaks Estate - Portage 78-79
The Barrister's House - Baraboo 80-81
House of Seven Gables - Baraboo 82-83
B&B House on River Road - Wisconsin Dells 84-85
Historic Bennett House - Wisconsin Dells 86-87
Sherman House - Wisconsin Dells 88-89
The Victorian Swan on Water - Stevens Point 90-91
Rosenberry Inn - Wausau 92-93

-East Wisconsin Waters 94-111
Area Map 94-95
McConnell Inn - Green Lake 96-97
Oakwood Lodge - Green Lake 98-99
Strawberry Hill B&B - Green Lake 100-101
The Farmer's Daughter Inn - Ripon 102-103
The Farm Homestead - New Holstein 104-105
52 Stafford, An Irish Guest House - Plymouth 106-107
The Parkside - Appleton 108-109
The Gables - Kewaunee 110-111

-Door County 112-139
Area Map 112-113
The Barbican - Sturgeon Bay 114-115
Bay Shore Inn - Sturgeon Bay 116-117
The Inn at Cedar Crossing - Sturgeon Bay 118-119
The Scofield House - Sturgeon Bay 120-121
The White Lace Inn - Sturgeon Bay 122-123
Thorp House Inn - Fish Creek 124-125
The Whistling Swan - Fish Creek 126-127
The White Gull Inn - Fish Creek 128-129
The French Country Inn - Ephraim 130-131
The Hillside Hotel - Ephraim 132-133
The Renaissance Inn - Sister Bay 134-135
The Griffin Inn - Ellison Bay 136-137
The Nelson Farm - Ellison Bay 138-139

-Hidden Valleys 140-165
Area Map 140-141
Just-N-Trails - Sparta 142-143
Lonesome Jake's Devil's Hole Ranch - Norwalk 144-145
Downings' B&B - Ontario 146-147
Dusk to Dawn B&B - Kendall 148-149
Trillium - LaFarge 150-151
Westby House - Westby 152-153
Serendipity Farm - Viroqua 154-155
Viroqua Heritage Inn - Viroqua 156-157
The Chesterfield Inn - Mineral Point 158-159
The Duke House - Mineral Point 160-161
The Jones House - Mineral Point 162-163
The Wisconsin House Stagecoach Inn - Hazel Green 164-165

-Southern Gateway & Milwaukee 166-209
Area Map 166-167
The Manor House - Kenosha 168-169
Foxmoor B&B - Wilmot 170-171
Eleven Gables On the Lake - Lake Geneva 172-173
Elizabethian Inn and the Kimberly House - Lake Geneva 174-175
The French Country Inn - Lake Geneva 176-177
Richardson House - Beloit 178-179
Jackson Street Inn - Janesville 180-181
Allyn House - Delavan 182-183
The Greene House - Whitewater 184-185
Greystone Farms - East Troy 186-187
Monches Mill House - Hartland 188-189
Fargo Mansion Inn - Lake Mills 190-191
The Collins House - Madison 192-193
Mansion Hill Inn - Madison 194-195
The Plough Inn - Madison 196-197
The Charly House - Horicon 198-199
Stagecoach Inn - Cedarburg 200-201
Washington House Inn - Cedarburg 202-203
American Country Farm - Mequon 204-205
Sonnenhof Inn - Mequon 206-207
Ogden House - Milwaukee 208-209

Extras .... *Groupings by Location, Name and Category, etc.* 210

Preface

Shame on me. I was raised in Michigan and have spent most of my adult life in Minnesota. I guess I knew that Wisconsin had to offer many of the things I loved about the two "M" states, but I'd never spent much time actually uncovering Wisconsin's assets. I now sheepishly admit that, until I went to write this book, Wisconsin was mostly a "sandwich state" to me: long stretches of 55 mph highway in between where I was and where I wanted to be.

But just like the famous chocolate "sandwich" cookie, there's lots of good stuff in the middle. This book gave me a reason to get off the main highways and travel the backroads. This past summer, the backroads *were* my destination.

The most pleasant surprise was the Hidden Valleys region in southwest Wisconsin. No region is more appropriately named. Those limestone peaks drop off to deep valleys, cut by clear creeks, along which roads wind. It's impossible -- and silly -- to go more than, say, 25 mph, on some of these scenic drives. And glimpses of the people added so much: a boy on his bike thanked a crossing guard, who winked as he sent the boy off; Amish farmers waved from buggies and patiently answered questions while selling their maple syrup; when radio reception came in at all in these valleys, it most likely was "WCOW, Cow Countre-e-e!" Stolen lawnmowers made the local news and a laundromat advertised that it has change machines.

There were many other Lake Wobegonish joys. "U-pick" raspberries in Bayfield were so huge and juicy that no one in the patch needed to move far to pick their fill. Devil's Lake State Park in Baraboo was a dramatic diversion from area farmland. Hot days in an un-air-coniditioned car were alleviated in the cool waters of Ike Walton Lake at Lac du Flambeau, complete with shallow, sandy beach. The Mexican food in Milwaukee is better than what I've eaten in Mexico (and without unpleasant after-effects). When I'd had enough of summer crowds, a beautiful, hot afternoon was spent on a secluded state park beach in Door County. And, having a bathroom at home in need of remodeling, I was sufficiently impressed by the stacks of Kohler sinks, tubs and toilets on display in Kohler.

And this is just the beginning. I want to go back and bike all of the Elroy-Sparta Bike Trail, visit the Wisconsin Historical Society museum in Madison and the giant muskie museum in Hayward, ride the steam engine trains near Baraboo, take in the American Players Theater in Spring Green, and see the geese migrating through Horicon. And do it all staying in B&Bs, of course. Wisconsin hooked me. I can only ask myself, "What took you so long?"

Introduction

What to Know about Using this Guide

For a very long time, it seemed that "getting away from it all" meant a week in the summer at the family cabin or at a resort housekeeping cottage.

But we have changed. Fewer people are waiting until retirement to enjoy traveling. More parents feel less guilty for making arrangements to leave the kids at home and getting away *from* them, instead of *with* them. Many two-career couples are so busy they rarely see each other.

We want to get away more often, for shorter periods of time, and stay closer to home. Three-day weekends now make up most of our "vacations."

And we want to treat ourselves. We don't seem to want super-slick city hotels or the stimulation of blaring TVs or ringing phones on these getaways. Instead, we're looking toward lodging in facilities that are warm and personal - right down to the decorating, the homey feeling often inspired by Early American decor and Victorian antiques. We want to return to a slower pace, if only for overnight. And we may want to rekindle some romance in a four-poster bed or a double whirlpool.

This book is intended as a guide to those getaways.

Why is this guide necessary?

This much credible information isn't available in any other single publication or in any consistent manner. Many of these establishments are very new and haven't been "written up" in articles or other guides. And most have limited advertising or public relations budgets, so they depend on word-of-mouth or an occasional feature story in a local paper to get out the word.

Also, many travelers don't know what B&Bs or country inns are, and many municipalities are giving prospective innkeepers a tremendously hard time because of ignorance. Perhaps this book will serve as an educational tool to spread the good news -- this is a *great* way to travel and a tourism asset in every community.

So, then, what is a B&B?

B&B stands for Bed and Breakfast. For years, travelers to Europe have enjoyed inexpensive accommodations in the extra bedroom of a local family. They found that B&Bs not only saved money and provided lodging in out-of-the-way places, but were a great way to meet friendly local people.

To say the B&B movement is catching on in America is a whopper of an understatement. The East and West coasts are loaded with them, and at least one glossy national magazine is devoted to B&Bs and country inns. In Wisconsin, historic B&Bs are not necessarily economical, but they definitely remain a good way to meet neighbors. And they are much different than a motel or hotel.

Wisconsin is one of the few states to have a legal definition of B&B establishments, having passed a law in 1983 which also spells out rules and regulations for operation of a B&B. It defines a bed-and-breakfast establishment as an owner-occupied place of lodging with four guest rooms or fewer. Also, it stipulates the only meal served to guests be breakfast.

The state Legislature, in recognizing this special category of lodgings in the 1983 law, has increased opportunities for operating B&B facilities in communities which otherwise might not have them. Since many B&B travelers travel on a B&B "circuit" and simply won't visit cities without B&Bs, the increased number of these accommodations surely has benefitted Wisconsin tourism. At the same time, it's helped preserve and restore many historic buildings which, otherwise, would be cut up into apartments, sit empty and deteriorate, or even be razed because they are no longer economical as single family homes. Also, certainly the business has helped supplement incomes in parts of the state where employment is seasonal or just plain hard-to-find. Some people grumble about the law -- particularly innkeepers with five guest rooms -- but Wisconsin lawmakers should be commended for their foresight and understanding of this new travel concept and its impact.

The law doesn't define a B&B any further, but here are some additional typical characteristics: a B&B often shares bathrooms and other common rooms, such as living and dining rooms, and includes some kind of breakfast in the room rate. It's common for guests to find themselves talking with other guests and the hosts in the living room at night, making arrangements to have dinner together, and sharing local travel tips as they pass the breakfast platter the next morning.

That won't happen in a motel or hotel room. And, unlike motels or hotels, each B&B is different. Most are cozy and homey. Guests are, afterall, sharing someone's home, which means guests are really guests and should act like such. Meeting the owners is part of the personalized service.

What is a country inn?

One Wisconsin innkeeper said he sometimes tells people who ask, "Have you ever seen Bob Newhart's show? It's kind of like the place he and Joanna run."

Kind of. A country inn, first of all, doesn't have to be in the country. What makes it "country" is more its size and atmosphere. It's larger than a B&B -- roughly eight rooms or more -- but smaller than a hotel. That means it has some of the personal atmosphere of a B&B with some of the privacy of a hotel. Some amenities, like phones or TVs in the room, are more likely than in B&Bs. Breakfast may or may not be included in the room rate. Also, rooms usually are in the same structure (most often upstairs) as the kitchen, lobby and dining areas.

Since licensing requirements are different, inns are more likely to serve meals other than breakfast. Innkeepers are often willing and able to put on splendid weddings or other private parties (so will some B&B owners, so ask!).

Guides for being a good guest

Most people who choose to travel this way are wonderful folks: quiet, easy-going and honest. It's rare, innkeepers say, to have a check bounce or find a towel missing. If you've never traveled this way, it might be helpful to point out a few hints that will ingratiate you with innkeepers.

The point, of course, is to feel at home. But remember it is someone else's home, and you are a guest. Don't call for reservations at midnight. Don't tie up their phone. Be courteous of other guests, especially if you smoke or are sharing bathrooms. Hosts will often provide advice and information on local activities and sites, but they are not your personal tour guides. Nor are they bellhops or providers of room service. Generally, if you honestly think you are a good guest when you visit friends or relatives, you will be a good B&B/inn traveler.

Who was selected to be included in this book?

First of all, only historic structures were included. "Historic" is roughly defined as 50 years or older and, hopefully, of some local historic significance. Several of the structures included in this guide are listed on the National Register of Historic Places, and all of them have interesting pasts.

Secondly, innkeepers were told their place needed to "feel" historic both inside and out. The history could be carried inside through Early American, Victorian or "country" decor or use of antiques. Therefore, historic homes or buildings which have been completely modernized and then turned into B&Bs were not included.

Unlike many guides, which make money both from readers buying the book and innkeepers paying to be included, no one paid to be in this book. This book is intended to provide credible information for the benefit of readers/travelers, not as an advertising vehicle for innkeepers. Not all historic B&Bs or inns were selected for inclusion (see below).

Each facility which was included was personally visited by the author. Please do not think this counts as any kind of "inspection," as cleanliness and any other aspect of service may vary. This book was intended as a guide to provide information, not an end-all-and-be-all ratings service. Cleanliness or other concerns about the way business is conducted should be reported to health, business and tourism officials.

Many of the innkeepers whose lodgings were selected for inclusion have spent long hours and lots of money in restoration, renovation and redecorating. Some have spent considerably less of all of the above. Which brings us to...

Opinion or, "Just the facts, ma'am?"

In most cases, if facilities met the above criteria, they were included. The writing was designed to simply describe the facilities of the B&B or inn, without many adjectives. Then readers could make their own choices according to their own tastes and preferences.

After the first "Room at the Inn," which covered Minnesota's historic B&Bs, hotels and country inns, some readers wanted more of the author's opinions. So in this book, the author tried to make clear which establishments and innkeepers were exceptional.

Who is not included?

Very few historic B&Bs or inns known to the author were left out. The reasons varied. A few historic structures were left out because they did not fit the above criteria: that is, they were too modernized on the outside or on the inside, or both.

Others did not seem to be the type of place which the audience of this book would want to visit, for various reasons. A few were left out because a visit could not be arranged or innkeepers did not want the publicity at this time. Doubtless, some were left out because the author was not aware of them.

Large hotels, resorts and wilderness lodges are not included, though there are many fine facilities available.

No reservation services have been included. Part of the fun of traveling this way is getting to know the hosts. Arrangements can be made directly with each of the innkeepers listed in this guide.

What readers should know about...

...Descriptions: On each facility, a short feature was written about the history of the inn, renovation or restoration efforts, and the innkeepers themselves. This was to give interesting background information about the facility and the people who run it. Historical information was provided by the innkeepers.

...Rooms: The number of rooms and some examples of decor and bathroom arrangements are explained. The space was very limited, so please ask innkeepers for more complete information.

...Rates: Rates are current for all of 1987 and well into 1988, in most cases. If in doubt, assume about 5 percent increase per year, with rates usually lower in winter. Of course, all rates are subject to change, and please do not call innkeepers nasty names if their rates have gone up.

How do you know if rates are fair? Generally, it's true that you get what you pay for. A few facilities are overpriced; a few are real bargains. Most are fairly priced. Innkeepers generally know how their "product" compares with other innkeepers, and there probably is a reason the price is so high or so low. The question becomes, can you live with that reason? (Private bathrooms are the most frequent reason for charging more; see the section on Shared Baths, next page.)

Expect to pay more for exceptional location, weekend or holiday travel, private baths, full breakfasts (though some aren't), extensive or expensive redecorating or restoration, whirlpools, fireplaces, air conditioners, color/cable TVs, and other amenities.

Expect to get a break on rates if you share a bath, are willing to stay a little ways out of town or travel midweek in off-peak seasons. Or choose places where innkeepers spent less on decorating and remodeling.

Because rates often have little in common with what guests will get at hotels or motels for the same rate, here's a very general breakdown on what guests might get for their money:

$65 and up - Privacy is sometimes what you're buying here, since many of the inns in this price range are designed as romantic or cozy weekend getaways. These are most often places for two types of travelers: those who can afford to travel this way, and those who are splurging for a memorable honeymoon, anniversary or birthday treat. The inns themselves have probably had major renovation and expert decoration, perhaps with designer linens or handmade quilts, for example. For this amount, something special usually is included, such as a bottle of wine and candies on the pillow at night, a private bath, air conditioning, and perhaps a whirlpool, working fireplace or lake view.

$35-$60 - These mid-priced lodgings may be worth every bit as much as the higher priced, except for one thing. Maybe they are located slightly out of town or in a town which won't support higher rates, or they have shared baths. Generally, this price range usually means something has been spent on tasteful decor and comfortable furnishings. And these are places that are smaller and opportunities are greater to sit on the porch swing and talk with other guests or the owners, or have them sit down at the breakfast table with you. Keep in mind that some older homes are so well-designed, located under big trees or with a lake breeze, so they really don't need air conditioning, for instance.

Under $35 - It's possible to find a few real deals here, B&Bs with pleasant rooms and hearty breakfasts. But if you get what you pay for, why are they charging less? Often it's because relatively little money has been put into converting the home into a B&B. That means shared baths, perhaps rugs instead of carpeting, painted walls instead of wallpapered, occasionally modern ceilings, and the living room has dad's easy chair instead of chintz-covered designer furniture. Sometimes this price range simply means that particular room is small, or the B&B is in an out-of-the-way spot that doesn't draw big tourism dollars. The low price doesn't mean the place isn't clean or otherwise perfectly OK.

...**Tax:** In addition to Wisconsin sales tax of 5 percent, many municipalities levy additional taxes. Some counties levy extra sales taxes and some municipalities also tack on a "bed tax" or "room tax," which overnight lodging facilities must charge. Commonly, that money is used to promote the community. Don't be surprised to have up to 10 percent total tax added to your bill.

About "shared baths:"

Can we talk? Let's be frank. Don't shy away from a place because you have to share a bathroom. It's not like you're traveling in Mexico, after all. Here, you'll miss some really nice places and people (plus lower rates) if you refuse to share.

Some people envision "shared bath" very literally, as if there were five or six people in there all at once. Not the case, of course, and most often there are only two or three rooms sharing. And some of those might not be rented, in which case you'll end up with a private bath, anyway.

If you share, simply be courteous of other guests (translation: if you walk around naked at home, please throw a robe on here). Also, a sink in the bedroom can be a big help; then teeth can be brushed without having to get in the shared bathroom.

...**Meals:** Breakfasts run the full gamut here, from serve-yourself continental to hearty breakfasts that will last you for hours. Note that "juice, tea, coffee" don't appear in the "meals" section because everyone offers them. Many times a choice of juices, milk and cocoa are offered, as well.

...**Dates open:** Almost every inn or B&B is open year 'round, but some are strictly seasonal, or offer a different experience in the less crowded "off season."

...**Smoking:** As more non-smokers are asserting themselves, more innkeepers are feeling less guilty and "just say no." Some inns allow smoking outside on porches only. Others don't want smokers to bother other guests so smoking is allowed only in the private guest rooms. Still others don't want the liability of people smoking in bed and don't allow it in guest rooms.

Innkeepers who smoke have been noted in this section, though some are not happy about it. It's really no problem in the summer, but it makes a difference to non-smokers who visit in the winter when the windows aren't open.

...**Children:** While some establishments welcome children, others are designed as weekend or special-event adult getaways. They are not set up for children of any age who may disturb other guests. Others simply don't have cribs or child-proof furnishings. Some may accept older children but require renting a separate room for them. On the other hand, even places that say "no children" may make an exception when they have room, so it doesn't hurt to ask.

...**Pets:** Even fewer lodgings will accept pets than will accept children. Still, there are those that do. Many innkeepers will make arrangements for your pet at a local kennel if you so request.

...**Nearby:** Major attractions and services within walking and driving distances are included. Some innkeepers keep brochures or local guides on hand for guests.

For more information before you leave home, contact
   • **Wisconsin Division of Tourism,** 1-800-ESCAPES
   (for Wisconsin and neighboring states), or 608-266-2161,
   P.O. Box 7606,
   Madison, WI 53703

Or contact the individual tourism regions:
- Indian Head Country, 800-472-6654 in Wisconsin, 800-826-6966 in neighboring states, P.O. Box 158, Altoona, WI 54720;
- Northwoods, 715-369-2330, P.O. Box 1167, Rhinelander, WI 54501;
- Central Wisconsin River Country, 608-339-3382, P.O. Box 308, Friendship, WI 53934;
- East Wisconsin Waters (including Door County), 414-494-9507, P.O. Box 10596, Green Bay, WI 54307;
- Hidden Valleys, 608-782-2467 P.O. Box 2527, LaCrosse, WI 54601;
- Southern Gateway, 414-273-0090, P.O. Box 451, Elm Grove, WI 53122;
- Greater Milwaukee, 414-273-7222 or 414-276-8482, Convention and Visitors Bureau, 756 N. Milwaukee St., Milwaukee, WI 53202.

Door County information also can be obtained through the Door County Chamber of Commerce, 414-743-4456; Box 346, Station A, Sturgeon Bay, WI 54235.

...Location/Directions: This section probably won't be helpful unless or until you are looking at a map or are in town trying to find the place. Driving times are approximate and will vary depending on starting points, road conditions and driving speed. Expect them to be reasonably accurate within a half-hour for summer driving at 55 mph.

...Deposit: Most innkeepers want a deposit to hold advance reservations. Ask about cancellation policies when making the reservation.

...Payment: Nearly every innkeeper will accept personal checks, so credit cards are not necessary. Small B&Bs often cannot afford the service charges by credit card companies, so they prefer to operate on a cash basis.

For more information, simply ask! This book provides an introduction to the innkeepers. You don't need to go through reservation services or travel agents -- just pick up the phone and call. They'll be happy to help you.

Happy traveling!

1. Cooper Hill House - Bayfield
2. Greunke's Inn - Bayfield
3. Grey Oak Guest House - Bayfield
4. Le Chateau Boutin - Bayfield
5. Old Rittenhouse Inn - Bayfield
6. Pinehurst Inn - Bayfield
7. Woods Manor B&B - LaPointe (Madeline Island)
8. Seven Pines Lodge - Lewis
9. The Mustard Seed - Hayward
10. The Stout Trout B&B - Springbrook
11. The Willson House - Chippewa Falls
12. Son-ne-Vale Farm - Colfax
13. St. Croix River Inn - Osceola
14. Jefferson-Day House - Hudson
15. The Yankee Bugler - Prescott
16. Great River Farm - Stockholm
17. Gallery House - Alma
18. The Laue House - Alma
19. The Inn - Montreal
20. Chippewa Lodge B&B - Lac du Flambeau
21. Cranberry Hill B&B Inn - Rhinelander
22. Glacier Wilderness B&B - Elton
23. Lauerman Guest House Inn - Marinette
24. By the Okeag Guest House - Columbus
25. Bonnie Oaks Estate - Portage
26. The Barrister's House - Baraboo
27. House of Seven Gables - Baraboo
28. B&B House on River Road - Wisconsin Dells
29. Historic Bennett House - Wisconsin Dells
30. Sherman House - Wisconsin Dells
31. The Victorian Swan on Water - Stevens Point
32. Rosenberry Inn - Wausau
33. McConnell Inn - Green Lake
34. Oakwood Lodge - Green Lake
35. Strawberry Hill B&B - Green Lake
36. The Farmer's Daughter Inn - Ripon
37. The Farm Homestead - New Holstein
38. 52 Stafford, An Irish Guest House - Plymouth
39. The Parkside - Appleton
40. The Gables - Kewaunee
41. The Barbican - Sturgeon Bay
42. Bay Shore Inn - Sturgeon Bay
43. The Inn at Cedar Crossing - Sturgeon Bay
44. The Scofield House - Sturgeon Bay
45. The White Lace Inn - Sturgeon Bay
46. Thorp House Inn - Fish Creek
47. The Whistling Swan - Fish Creek
48. The White Gull Inn - Fish Creek
49. The Hillside Hotel - Ephraim
50. The French Country Inn - Ephraim
51. The Renaissance Inn - Sister Bay
52. The Griffin Inn - Ellison Bay
53. The Nelson Farm - Ellison Bay
54. Just-N-Trails - Sparta
55. Lonesome Jake's Devil's Hole Ranch
56. Downings' B&B - Ontario
57. Dusk to Dawn B&B - Kendall
58. Trillium - LaFarge
59. Westby House - Westby
60. Serendipity Farm - Viroqua.
61. Viroqua Heritage Inn - Viroqua
62. The Chesterfield Inn - Mineral Point
63. The Duke House - Mineral Point
64. The Jones House - Mineral Point
65. Wisconsin House Stagecoach Inn
66. The Manor House - Kenosha
67. Foxmoor B&B - Wilmot
68. Eleven Gables On the Lake - Lake Geneva
69. Elizabethian Inn - Lake Geneva
70. The French Country Inn - Lake Geneva
71. Richardson House - Beloit
72. Jackson Street Inn - Janesville
73. Allyn House - Delavan
74. The Greene House - Whitewater
75. Greystone Farms - East Troy
76. Monches Mill House - Hartland
77. Fargo Mansion Inn - Lake Mills
78. The Collins House - Madison
79. Mansion Hill Inn - Madison
80. The Plough Inn - Madison
81. The Charly House - Horicon
82. Stagecoach Inn - Cedarburg
83. Washington House Inn - Cedarburg
84. American Country Farm - Mequon
85. Sonnenhof Inn - Mequon
86. Ogden House - Milwaukee

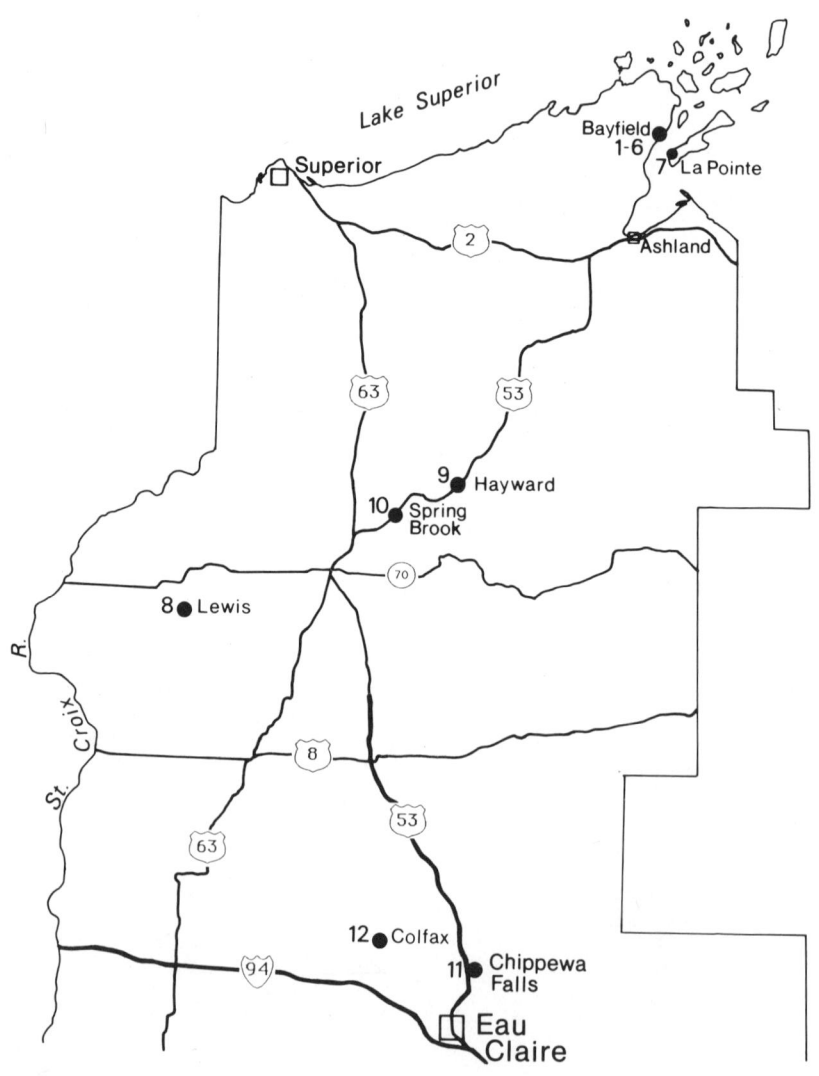

-Indian Head Country - North

1. Cooper Hill House - Bayfield.. 24-25
2. Greunke's Inn - Bayfield.. 26-27
3. Grey Oak Guest House - Bayfield... 28-29
4. Le Chateau Boutin - Bayfield.. 30-31
5. Old Rittenhouse Inn - Bayfield.. 32-33
6. Pinehurst Inn - Bayfield.. 34-35
7. Woods Manor B&B - LaPointe (Madeline Island)................................ 36-37
8. Seven Pines Lodge - Lewis... 38-39
9. The Mustard Seed - Hayward.. 40-41
10. The Stout Trout B&B - Springbrook... 42-43
11. The Willson House - Chippewa Falls.. 44-45
12. Son-ne-Vale Farm B&B - Colfax... 46-47

Bayfield

Cooper Hill House
33 S. Sixth St.
P.O. Box 5
Bayfield, WI 54814
715-779-5060

Owners/Operators:
Sheree and Phil Peterson

"I'd always gone by this house and thought, 'Geez, what you could do with a house like this,' " said Phil Peterson. What you could do, he and Sheree, his wife, and a partner found out, is reroof, insulate, replumb, change doorways, add bathrooms, and paint the place yellow.

But now that that's done, the Petersons (who have since bought out their partner) get to live in the 1888 home and meet lots of nice visitors who want to stay there, too. The home is about eight blocks from Lake Superior on Cooper Hill, named after a local family. The hill was a favorite for bobsledding in the early 1900s.

For materials, the original builders, Mary and Martin Johnson, used hemlock and white pine from Henry Wachsmuth's lumberyard. Johnson was a millwright there, but later his employer would own the home, purchasing it as a wedding gift for his son. Wachsmuth was a young entrepreneur, having opened his lumber company at age 25. His descendents owned the home until Petersons bought it with Rick Thompson in the fall of 1983. The B&B opened in June 1984.

Phil Peterson came to Bayfield in 1977 as a manager for a sailboat charter; Sheree came in 1978 as a park service employee. All furnishings in their B&B are antiques; the dining room buffet came from a home on one of the Apostle Islands. The bathroom sinks were purchased from the Curtis Hotel in Minneapolis before it was demolished - look underneath to see where Phil has written the room number from which the sink came. Guests may use the living and dining rooms, the large porch and the yard, with lawn chairs.

Rooms and Rates: Four - All with private baths, done in antiques with Curtis Hotel sinks. Rose Room - queen brass bed, shower - $55. Brass Room - double bed, shower only - $55. Green Room - white iron double bed, shower and tub - $55. Bittersweet Room, brass double bed with oak trim, view of Long Island light at night, shower only - $50. $3 less for singles. Add tax. Off-season discounts.

Meals: Continental breakfast is served in the dining room 8-9:45 and includes fresh fruit, homemade muffins or breads, homemade jams.

Dates open: May - October; winter by reservation   **Pets:** No

Smoking: On front porch only   **Children:** "At parents' discretion"

Nearby: Located in Bayfield historic district. Headquarters to Apostle Islands National Lakeshore, 3 blocks. Ferry to Madeline Island, excursion boats, marina, shops, restaurants, 5-8 blocks. Big Top Chautauqua (lecturers, music, programs) in summer, 7 miles. Downhill and x-c skiing.

Location/Directions: Highway 13 turns into Sixth Street in town, house is on the left with sign. Chicago, 8.5 hours. Madison, 6 hours. Milwaukee, 7 hours. Twin Cities, 4.5 hours.

Deposit: Half of room rate

Payment: Cash, personal or traveler's checks, VISA or MasterCard

Bayfield

Greunke's Inn
17 Rittenhouse Ave.
P.O. Box 768
Bayfield, WI 54814
715-779-5480

Owners/Operators:
Judith Lokken-Strom and Alan Waite

Nazar LaBonte was a French-Canadian who ended up in Bayfield, but not by choice. Having lost his money while gambling on board a ferry from Detroit to Superior, Wis., the crew off-loaded him in LaPointe on Madeline Island in the early 1860s.

Making the best of a bad situation, LaBonte went to work logging off the Bayfield peninsula, and soon opened the "LaBonte House," explains Alan Waite. The boarding house was downtown in Bayfield's busiest intersection and operated until the 1920s.

Eventually modernized and converted to a restaurant downstairs, the place achieved a pleasing reputation under the ownership of Vic and Irene Greunke, who bought it in the 1940s and ran a restaurant and inn until 1975. Greunke's Inn was the local gathering spot, and rooms upstairs often went to fishermen and hunters.

Judith and Alan now run the inn and restaurant. In 1983, they did some remodeling, including adding bathrooms to some rooms. Putting in new fiberboard ceilings and baths, wallpapering and furnishing with antiques acquired through the years, they have maintained one of the oldest continuously operating businesses in Bayfield. The layout of the upstairs guest rooms remains essentially the same as in Nazar LaBonte's day.

During the summer months, Greunke's has added a traditional Wisconsin fish boil to its menu, which already includes Lake Superior fish.

Rooms and Rates: Seven, and one two-bedroom apartment - Two showers and a half-bath in the hall; some rooms with half-baths. All can use porch with lake view. Examples include #1 with blonde birdseye maple antique double and twin beds, done in yellows, shares bath. #3 has an antique wooden queen with half-bath, done in tan and rose. The apartment has one bedroom, a loft, a bathroom with shower, TV and kitchen. $30 - $50, depending on season. Add tax.

Meals: Full breakfast menu available in the restaurant downstairs, which is open 6 a.m.-10 p.m. daily.

Dates open: Mid-April through mid-October

Smoking and Pets: "Not encouraged"   **Children:** Yes (under 6 free)

Nearby: Located in Bayfield historic district. Headquarters to Apostle Islands National Lakeshore, 5 blocks. Ferry to Madeline Island, excursion boats, marina, shops, restaurants, 1-2 blocks. Big Top Chautauqua (lecturers, music, programs) in summer, 7 miles. Downhill and x-c skiing.

Location/Directions: Follow Highway 13 through town; Greunke's on left at main intersection downtown. Chicago, 8.5 hours. Madison, 6 hours. Milwaukee, 7 hours. Twin Cities, 4.5 hours.

Deposit: Half of room rate

Payment: Cash, personal or traveler's checks, VISA or MasterCard

Bayfield

Grey Oak Guest House

Seventh and Manypenny
P.O. Box 584
Bayfield, WI 54814
715-779-5111

Operator:
    Old Rittenhouse Inn
Innkeepers:
    Susan Larsen and Neil Howk

Ervin Leighy was one businessman who had a vision for Bayfield's future, a future that the town would survive past the lumbering, brownstone quarrying and fishing era of the late 1800s and early 1900s.

And he put his money where his mouth was: his residence had a full brownstone foundation, guaranteed to last practically forever.

The 1888 home was built on what was then the outskirts of town. Now, the house is within the Bayfield Historic District and what might be considered the middle of town, though Bayfield has only 800 residents.

The home stayed in the Leighy family until the 30s, when it was acquired by the Hadland family. Eventually, an apartment was constructed on the second floor, but the home remained otherwise structurally unchanged.

When the Hadland family wanted to sell, Susan Larsen was interested. She and her husband had come to Bayfield as National Park Service employees. Susan since began work for Mary and Jerry Phillips at the Old Rittenhouse Inn. A partnership was formed to buy, redo and rent the house, the third property run by the Old Rittenhouse Inn.

While some of the original floors remain, major renovation was necessary. Walls were rebuilt to make three large guest rooms, new plumbing was added, the house was insulated and rewired, and fireplaces were added.

Guests have use of the living room with fireplace and front porch.

Rooms and Rates: Three - All with private bath with tubs and showers, queen sized brass beds and fireplaces. Upstairs is a two-room suite with a sofa bed, done in mauve and green - $99. Downstairs are two rooms, one in cranberry with hardwood floors, and the other in grey and mauve, both $89. Add tax.

Meals: Continental breakfast included, by reservation at the Old Rittenhouse Inn, 4 blocks away. Full breakfast available.

Dates open: May - October; some weekends rest of winter

Smoking: Yes   **Pets:** No   **Children:** Yes

Nearby: Located in Bayfield historic district. Headquarters to Apostle Islands National Lakeshore, 5 blocks. Excursion boats and ferry to Madeline Island, marina, restaurants and shops, 7-9 blocks. Big Top Chautauqua (lecturers, music, programs) in summer, 7 miles. Downhill and x-c skiing.

Location/Directions: Highway 13 to town. Turn left on either 7th or Manypenny to corner. Chicago, 8.5 hours. Madison, 6 hours. Milwaukee, 7 hours. Twin Cities, 4.5 hours.

Deposit: First night's lodging

Payment: Cash, personal or traveler's checks, VISA or MasterCard

Bayfield

Le Chateau Boutin

7 Rice Street
P.O. Box 584
Bayfield, WI 54814
715-779-5111

Owners/Operators:
Mary and Jerry Phillips,
Greg Carrier

This National Register of Historic Places home was built in 1907 for lumber baron Frank Boutin, Jr., who used it as a year 'round family home. Boutin was a busy Bayfield businessman, also starting a fishing fleet. Despite touches like detailed stained and leaded glass, Boutin's wife didn't like life in Bayfield, and they moved to California after five years in the home.

The Elmore family of Chicago then used the place as a summer home, adding formal gardens, but it was lost in the stock market crash.

Early on, a clause put into the sales agreement stated ownership would revert to the local Catholic church should the home be foreclosed upon. The church assumed ownership several times over the next decades, finally using it as a convent for nuns who taught at the local school.

Paul Turner bought it from the church in the '70s, providing a bit more local color and excitement than the good sisters had. Turner renamed it The Mansion, rented rooms and gave tours, which sometimes included his playing a massive organ from the third floor ballroom.

In failing health, Turner sold to the new owners. They opened the B&B in July 1985 after extensive renovation. The original seven-leaf mahogany Chippendale dining room table, imported from Paris, remains from Boutin's era, as does the stained and leaded glass throughout the home.

Guests have use of the living room with fireplace, the music room and the huge porch, and get a tour of the home.

Rooms and Rates: Six - All with private bath, five with fireplaces. Examples include: the North East Room, with a double door to porch, an original black walnut bed with angels carved to guard sleepers, fireplace - $89. The Tower Room is done in tiger birch, double bed - $69. Turret Suite is former men's poker room plus women's game room, with seven windows and sitting room, king brass bed - $99. Third floor South Room in blue and white has sloping ceilings, queen bed - $79. Add tax.

Meals: Continental breakfast included, by reservation at the Old Rittenhouse Inn, 4 blocks away. Full breakfast available.

Dates open: May - October; some weekends rest of winter

Smoking: Yes   **Pets:** No   **Children:** Yes

Nearby: Located in Bayfield historic district. Headquarters to Apostle Islands National Lakeshore, 4 blocks. Excursion boats and ferry to Madeline Island, marina, restaurants, shops, 3--6 blocks. Big Top Chautauqua (lecturers, music, programs) in summer, 7 miles. Downhill and x-c skiing.

Location/Directions: Follow Highway 13 almost out of town, turn left on Rice. Chicago, 8.5 hours. Madison, 6 hours. Milwaukee, 7 hours. Twin Cities, 4.5 hours.

Deposit: First night's lodging

Payment: Cash, personal or traveler's checks, VISA or MasterCard

Bayfield

Old Rittenhouse Inn

Rittenhouse and Third
P.O. Box 584
Bayfield, WI 54814
715-779-5111

Owners/Operators:
Mary and Jerry Phillips

When Mary and Jerry Phillips opened a B&B in a Bayfield mansion in the summer of 1974, they didn't know that's what they were doing. The concept hadn't reached the Midwest yet. "The place had been used as a boarding house at one time, and we were getting calls since there was a shortage of rooms in town," Jerry said. "We said, 'Maybe we should take a couple rooms a night.' " Food lovers that they are, they soon added gourmet breakfasts.

Today, the Old Rittenhouse Inn is a nine-room country inn, expanded once, with elegant dining on the first floor. The Phillips also operate two other Bayfield B&Bs, Grey Oak Guest House and LeChateau Boutin.

While teaching music in Madison, the couple bought the 26-room 1890 summer home of Civil War Gen. Allen Fuller, going against the advice of friends and relatives. "They thought we were nuts," Jerry said. "We simply bought it because we fell in love with the house. It was 1973, kerosene was 18 cents a gallon, and we thought we'd come up a couple times in the winter."

Restoration and filling the inn with antiques, plus the energy crisis and a few other factors, led to the need for a decision to be or not to be full-time innkeepers. After a sabbatical and visiting country inns in the East, they opted for Bayfield. Eventually lunches and dinners were added, and meals became more elaborate; Mary is still chef. Five guest rooms were added in 1984. A mail-order business has been started to offer preserves and other treats.

Rooms and Rates: Nine - All with private bath and antiques or reproductions; eight have working fireplaces; $59, $79 or $89. Examples include: Room 1, with original antique bed from the Fuller home and a lakeview - $59. Room 3 has lake view, original sink bowl and shower only - $79. Room 4 has a king bed with headboard goes to the ceiling - $89. Room 6 has white iron and brass bed, balcony - $89. Two rooms on first floor have wheelchair access. Each additional person, $15. Add tax.

Meals: Continental breakfast included by reservation: fresh fruit, homemade breads with homemade preserves. Full breakfast available. Open to the public for dinner nightly and Sunday brunch. Group luncheons/tours by arrangement.

Dates open: May - October; weekends rest of winter; closed January

Smoking: Yes   **Children:** Yes   **Pets:** No

Nearby: Located in Bayfield historic district. Headquarters to Apostle Islands National Lakeshore, excursion boats and ferry to Madeline Island, marina, restaurants and shops, 2 blocks. Big Top Chautauqua (lecturers, music, programs) in summer, 7 miles. Downhill and x-c skiing.

Location/Directions: Highway 13 turns into Rittenhouse Avenue downtown. Inn is on the left. Chicago, 8.5 hours. Madison, 6 hours. Milwaukee, 7 hours. Twin Cities, 4.5 hours.

Deposit: First night's lodging

Payment: Cash, personal or traveler's checks, VISA or MasterCard

Bayfield

Pinehurst Inn

Rt. 1, Box 222
Bayfield, WI 54814
715-779-3676

Owners/Operators:
Michele and Keith Ochsner

Despite six months of work before the family opened their B&B, not all family members were playing on the same team. No sooner had Keith Ochsner hung out the Pinehurst Inn shingle with the help of two young sons and returned to the basement when the first customers pulled in. The boys glared at them and one warned, "You get out of here." They did.

After a fatherly chat, the tables turned. It was the busy July 4th weekend, 1983, and "we were full in 20 minutes with the woodwork still tacky from the turpentine and linseed oil."

The 1895 structure had looked much different six months before, after years of disuse, when Ochsners became the third owners. Floors were leveled, walls replastered, ceilings redone, bathrooms added and rewiring and redecorating finished.

This is the home's second round of innhood. The second owner offered meals at the house for people staying in cabins on the beach across the highway. "There was an extra charge for electricity and guests had to provide references," Keith said. That ended abruptly during a freak flood in 1942, when 8.52 inches of rain in 12 hours caused the nearby creek to wash the beach cabins out into Lake Superior. There was a daring night-time rescue in which people in the cabins crawled up to the roof tops to be saved.

The first owner, who never rented rooms, was R.D. Pike. Wealthy sawmill owner Pike had the home designed by William Price, a Philadelphia architect. Only about 15 of his buildings are still standing; this one is on the National Register of Historic Places. Guests may use the living room with fireplace, library and dining room, porch, lawn, picnic tables and garden.

Rooms and Rates: Four - Room 1 has lake view, two queen beds, done in greens and browns with mallards on the wallpaper, private bath with clawfoot tub and sitting room - $65. Room 2 has king bed, done in blue with x-c skiiers, clawfoot tub and private bath - $50. Room 3 has queen bed, done in blue with seashell motif - $45. Room 4 has a double brass bed, light blues - $40. Rooms 3 and 4 share bath with tub and shower. Add tax.

Meals: Breakfast is served family-style in the dining room at 8:30 and may include fresh fruit in season, waffles, French Toast, pancakes, quiche or scrambled eggs.

Dates open: Year 'round   **Smoking:** "Ambivalent"

Children: Yes   **Pets:** Yes

Nearby: DNR fish hatchery, next door. Walk to Lake Superior, across highway. Ski hill and groomed x-c ski trails. Ferry dock and Bayfield shops, restaurants, etc., 2.5 miles. Big Top Chautauqua (lecturers, music, programs) in summer, 4 miles.

Location/Directions: Follow Highway 13 north about 17 miles from Ashland. Inn is on the left, right before the fish hatchery. Chicago, 8.5 hours. Madison, 6 hours. Milwaukee, 7 hours. Twin Cities, 4.5 hours.

Deposit: First night's lodging

Payment: Cash, personal or traveler's checks, VISA or MasterCard

LaPointe/Madeline Island

Woods Manor B&B

P.O. Box 7
LaPointe, WI 54850
715-747-3102

Owners/Operators:
Gail and Woody Petersen

This Madeline Island B&B is still in the family of the original owner. Woody Petersen is the great-grandson of the builder, F.H. Woods, a Lincoln, Nebraska, man.

Woods first came to Madeline Island with his father in the late 1800s, looking for relief from asthma or hay fever. Woods became acquainted with a Missourian, Hunter Gary, and the two went into business together after hearing about a new telephone device invented by an angry mortician.

The mortician, Woody Petersen explains, was angry at telephone operators. When the mortician's best friend died, the operator had switched the call for the business of embalming and burying the friend to a competitor. So, to eradicate powerful operators, the mortician devised the telephone dial. "He just wanted revenge," Petersen says, so he allowed Woods and Gary to patent the device, which they did, and very successfully at that. The two became neighbors on Madeline Island.

Woods built Woods Manor in the early 1920s with huge timber ceiling beams and plaster walls with oval window frames, resembling Mediterranean decor. He had a 140-foot yacht with which he toured the Apostle Islands. Both Coolidge and Pershing were acquaintances and they visited.

The Petersens opened the manor as a B&B in July 1985. Guests have use of the huge living room with a grand piano from the 1920s, porch and dining room with fireplaces in each, stereo system, satellite TV and swimming. The grounds stretch to the lake and a clay tennis court is in back. An outdoor hot tub bubbles off the living room and Woody has installed a sauna. Bikes are available free for guests' use.

Rooms and Rates: Six - All with private baths, four with shower only. Upstairs: One room has king-sized brass bed, tub and shower. Two rooms have antique provincial twin beds, one has shower only, other has tub and shower. One room has a double bed. Downstairs: One room has king bed, shower only. One room has queen bed, shower only. $50 May 1-21 and Oct. 4-winter; $65 May 22-July 2 and Sept. 7-Oct. 3; $75 July 3-Sept. 6. Add tax.

Meals: Continental breakfast is served in the dining room 8-10 and includes rolls, fresh fruit, coffee cakes and cold cereals.

Dates open: Year 'round   **Children:** Yes

Smoking: Yes   **Pets:** Check with owner

Nearby: Ferry dock, shops, restaurants, museum, municipal tennis courts in LaPointe, 3 blocks. Golf course with rental clubs, 3/4 mile. Swimming, sailing, windsurfing, hiking, biking, camping, beachcombing, x-c skiing on island.

Location/Directions: Follow Highway 13 to the ferry dock; ferries accept vehicles or they can be left in Bayfield parking lot. Off ferry, turn left and follow road along homes to Woods Manor (within walking distance of ferry). Chicago, 9 hours. Madison, 6.5 hours. Milwaukee, 7.5 hours. Twin Cities, 5 hours.

Deposit: Half of room rate

Payment: Cash, personal or traveler's checks, VISA or MasterCard

Lewis

Seven Pines Lodge
Lewis, WI 54851
715-653-2323

Owners/Operators:
Joan and David Simpson

Guests at this country inn will be surprised to find such a secluded forest hideaway. This is the fishing retreat of Charles Lewis, a Minneapolis man who owned a stock brokerage and grain exchange. Lewis bought 1530 acres from a St. Croix steamboat operator threatening to sell the virgin white pine to loggers. Lewis had been coming to fish the little trout stream and he loved the pines.

In the winter of 1903, he turned a few acres into a magnificent log estate: a main lodge, a stream house, an office by the gate (complete with a tickertape machine so he could do business), a garage and a glass-roofed swimming pool of hand-laid tiles, two dairy farms and several trout ponds. All are still there except the dairies and pool house.

Lewis' wife sold it after his death in 1932. Now, several owners later, it's owned by Joan and David Simpson, but Lewis would still feel at home. Many original furnishings remain. One reason the lodge is on the National Register of Historic Places is because President Calvin Coolidge once stayed there on his way north. The other is its architecture. Huge screened porches, solid log beams, a log stairway, a giant fireplace and wainscotting ceilings make it cozy. The stream house has a porch around all four sides, like a top-heavy fort.

Today, fishermen buy memberships to fish year 'round (there's no license or limit on the private, stocked stream). Overnight guests can fish for $15 extra, then must join to fish again. But they can order trout for dinner (or breakfast). The lodge only is open in the winter for groups of 10 or more to x-c ski. Groups rent it for retreats, weddings and mystery weekends. Rascal, the cat, will spend a night in a guestroom, and Moses, the yellow Lab, will take guests on a tour of the property.

Rooms and Rates: Five in Main Lodge, including the room President and Mrs. Coolidge stayed in, ranging from $54.95-$67.95; some share bath, extra shower room available, twins and doubles. Also gate ($74.95) and stream ($67.95) houses open in summer. Add tax. Off-season group rates.

Meals: Continental breakfast included; three meals by reservation. Joan cooks a selection of two or three dinners. Expect homemade breads, jams. Meals open to public by reservation.

Dates open: Year 'round; winter for groups of 10 or more only

Smoking: Not in rooms   **Children:** Yes   **Pets:** No

Nearby: Trout fishing and x-c skiing on 10 miles of trails out the door. Close to canoe rentals, hot air balloon rides, sugar bushes, cheese factories, pottery, art and antique shops, Crex Meadows Wildlife Refuge on the St. Croix River.

Location/Directions: Highway 35 north through Frederic to Lewis, go into town past the game farm and out the gravel road. Directions sent. Chicago, 9 hours. Madison, 6 hours. Milwaukee, 7.5 hours. Twin Cities, 1.5 hours.

Deposit: First night's lodging (note: reservations are required)

Payment: Cash, personal or traveler's checks only

Hayward

The Mustard Seed
205 California Ave.
P.O. Box 262
Hayward, WI 54843
715-634-2908

Owners/Operators:
Joanne and Roy Fadness

Built in 1901, this home in Hayward was owned twice over the years by the Quail family. Just two blocks from Highway 63, it was probably better remembered in town as the home of a veterinarian who lived there for 28 years.

Over the years, two fireplaces were put in and in 1953 a bedroom wing was added. In 1985, major work was done by Retta and Laurie Dixon, a mother-daughter team, who bought it to open as the Mustard Seed B&B. A new furnance, roof, wiring, plumbing, carpeting and windows ("We couldn't even get some of them open," Retta said) were all put in, as well as redecorating.

In August 1987, Joanne and Roy Fadness bought the business. They grew up in the Hayward area, and owned the Sears store and the Kentucky Fried Chicken in town. Joanne's great-grandparents were among the first settlers in the county.

A number of factors led the Fadnesses to buy an operating B&B. They had traveled out East and gone up the East Coast staying in inns and B&Bs, Joanne said, and she's worked in the hotel-motel business, so she knew they could do the work required. And, since they've spent so much time in Hayward, they know the area and can be a resource for guests. But, as businesspeople, it had a big appeal to them as a small business. "It's small enough to really associate with people," she said. Joanne wants to retire into the B&B business, one that still includes lots of human contact.

Guests will have a refrigerator with soft drinks and juice, and may use the living and dining rooms downstairs, plus the garden and back yard. Cookies are available in the afternoons, and the coffee pot is on all the time.

Rooms and Rates: Five - Four rented at once. All upstairs. Evergreen Room has two built-in twin bunks with knotty pine paneling. Cranberry Room has double bed, cranberry and cream wallpaper. Blue Room has double antique white iron bed, rag rug. Peach Room has queen bed, peach floral wallpaper. Up to three of these four rooms rented at once and share bath with tub and shower. $37.50 single, $40 double. Rosewood Suite has two-sided fireplace, queen bed, private bath with tub and shower - $60. Add tax. Winter discounts.

Meals: Continental breakfast is served in the dining room, kitchen or to the rooms from 8-9:30. It may include fresh seasonal fruit, homemade muffins or breads, jams and jellies.

Dates open: Year 'round   **Smoking:** In designated areas

Children: Over 11   **Pets:** No

Nearby: Lake Hayward (municipal beach), 4 blocks. Golf and tennis, 4 blocks. Downhill and x-c skiing, 17 miles. X-c skiing (Birkebeiner trail), 1.5 miles. Horseback riding, 4 miles. Fishing, sailing, boating, swimming within 5 miles or at Round Lake, 8 miles.

Location/Directions: Two blocks off Highway 63, turn onto California at the Holiday Station. Chicago, 8.5 hours. Madison, 5.5 hours. Milwaukee, 7 hours. Twin Cities, 3 hours.

Deposit: Half of room rate

Payment: Cash, personal or traveler's checks, VISA or MasterCard

Springbrook

The Stout Trout B&B

Route 1, Box 1630
Springbrook, WI 54875
715-466-2790

Owner/Operator:
Kathleen Fredricks

Trout fishermen wouldn't recognize the inside of the old Stilson resort on a corner of Gull Lake between Hayward and Spooner. Neither would the folks who patronized what was, according to local legend, a speakeasy during Prohibition.

Kathleen Fredricks took a year to find the place she wanted to turn into a B&B. And when she saw this old resort lodge, she saw beneath the Spanish Mediterranean decor, complete with Elvis paint-on-velvet, to the possibilities for a country B&B with wood plank floors, antiques and a lake view.

Fredricks traveled in B&Bs and lived in Europe, and then moved to the Sonoma Valley, Calif., where the B&B business is booming. When she wanted to return to Wisconsin (she grew up on a farm 60 miles away), she felt a B&B was a good tourist-oriented business.

After a year of seeing old buildings, she purchased this in January 1986, mostly because it had the required space and location. Gull Lake is well known for large mouth bass and northern pike fishing. The area is renown for trout fishing. Hayward has the annual Birkebeiner x-c ski marathon and an excellent system of x-c ski trails. The Stout Trout has a cottage remodeled just for storing waders and equipment and has fly-tying gear. A x-c ski waxing station is downstairs. Rowboats, a paddleboat and canoes are available for guests' use.

Inside, about all that could be saved was the kitchen, the doors and the wood floors. Workers told her the beams were unstable, and the upstairs was dark and uninsulated. Fredricks had them put in new ceilings, a roof, walls, plumbing, wiring, insulation and a furnace. Every room was repainted and redecorated with collections of antiques and linens, and Stout Trout opened in February 1987.

The B&B is on 40 acres of woods and fields, which guests are welcome to hike or ski. The home has two sun decks. Guests also have use of the large living and dining rooms downstairs, and may bring skis onto the back porch.

Rooms and Rates: Four - All upstairs with wood plank floors, individual thermostats, private baths with tubs and showers. Blue room has double antique bed, lake view. Red room has queen brass bed, twig chair, lake view. Green room has wicker double bed, handmade quilt, lake view. Brown room has double bed, animal prints on the walls, Navajo rug. $40 single, $45 double. Add tax.

Meals: Breakfast is served in the dining room or on the deck at a time arranged the night before. The menu is heavier in the cooler months; it may include homemade popovers or muffins with homemade jams, pancakes or waffles with homemade maple syrup, and fresh ground coffee.

Dates open: Year 'round

Smoking: Outside only

Children: Check with owner

Pets: No

Nearby: Trout fishing on Namekagon River, 5 miles, or Bean Brook, 6 miles. Canoeing, tubing also on Namekagon. X-c skiing on ungroomed trails, out the door; groomed trails, 6 miles. Birkebeiner x-c race, 15 miles. Horseback riding, 3 miles. Restaurants in Trego, 6 miles, or Hayward or Spooner, 15 miles. Berry picking, hiking, biking.

Location/Directions: From either Highway 53 or 63, take County Road F about 3 miles to Stout Trout sign. Chicago, 8.5 hours. Madison, 5.5 hours. Milwaukee, 7 hours. Twin Cities, 2.5 hours.

Deposit: None for one-night stays; first night's lodging for longer stays

Payment: Cash, personal or traveler's checks only

Chippewa Falls

The Willson House
320 Superior St.
Chippewa Falls, WI 54729
715-723-0055

Owners/Operators:
Barb and Tom Knowlton

It's easy for townsfolk not to like the richest businessmen in town, especially the ones who build mansions with dance halls on the third floor, single lane bowling alleys in the basement, and taking up a half-block of land.

But by all accounts, Leslie Willson, builder of this home 100-some years ago, often helped in civic projects but rarely grabbed the limelight. After growing up in Winona, Minn., Willson worked at a lumber company, sold teas and spices, and settled in Chippewa Falls. There he built up a wholesale grocery business. He was concerned with more than his company, and encouraged development in the city. When he died in 1906, every store in town closed to honor him for a day.

Nellie, his wife, plunged into running Chippewa Valley Mercantile after her husband's death. For 30 years, she lived alone in the big house (they had no children) and operated the business. Upon her death, a sister in California came back only long enough to sell the house, furniture and all.

Four other families owned the house as a single-family home, and then it sat empty for a year before Knowltons bought it in August 1986. "We weren't even looking for a house at the time," said Barb, who insisted they go through it anyway after the "for sale" sign was posted. "The realtor gave us the idea for a B&B."

In the 12 rooms, Tom, Barb and their 16-year-old son, who mows the gigantic lawn, put in new ceilings, replaced plumbing, removed the old wallpaper and replaced it with country and Victorian designs, and installed new carpets. They shopped estate sales for furnishings with such fury that their son is still shaking his head. Some of the renovation has been recorded in a photo album. Officially open in May 1987, guests can use the massive living room, dining room, porch and TV room, and bikes are available for use.

Rooms and Rates: Four - All upstairs. Front room has single antique bed, done in pinks and burgundy - $25. Other front room has queen bed with white wicker headboard and lace spread, private half-bath with stained glass window and fireplace - $40. Beige room has double antique bed - $35. Grey and peach room has giant antique headboard on double bed, sink and clawfoot tub (no shower) in room - $35. Shared bath down the hall has clawfoot tub and shower, reproduction pull-chain toilet, done in dark green and wood. Add tax. Business discounts.

Meals: Continental breakfast is set out on the buffet in the dining room at 8:30 or as arranged, and includes sweet rolls, fruit and cereal.

Dates open: Year 'round   **Smoking:** In living room only

Children: Over 12   **Pets:** No

Nearby: Cook-Rutledge Mansion tours, 1 block. Downtown restaurants and shops, 4 blocks. Jacob Leinenkugel brewery tours, Irvine Park (small zoo, picnic grounds, hiking and bike trails), both 2.5 miles. Lake Wissota (beaches, boat rentals), 6 miles.

Location/Directions: From I-94, take Highway 29. Turn left and go up the hill after going under the railroad bridge; go straight at the top for four blocks, house on the right. Chicago, 6.5 hours. Madison, 3.5 hours. Milwaukee, 5 hours. Twin Cities, 2 hours.

Deposit: $20-$25, depending on room

Payment: Cash, personal or traveler's checks only

Colfax

Son-ne-vale Farm B&B

Route 1, Box 132
Colfax, WI 54730
715-962-4343

Owner/Operator:
Lilyan Sonnenberg

"Peace and quiet" is the reason B&B guests come to Son-ne-vale Farm, says Lilyan Sonnenberg.

Originally, this valley was settled by the Anderson family, Norwegian immigrants. Ander Frome was the patriarch, immigrating in the mid-1800s. During the lumbering era, his four sons left their father's farm in the fall to join the logging camps, bringing home enough money for clothes and seed for spring planting.

The sons, eager to be Americanized, changed their surname to Anderson, bought adjoining farms and raised families. The valley was known locally as Anderson Valley.

During the hard Depression years, Son-ne-vale Farm was lost to the federal land bank, from whom Lilyan and the late Van Sonnenberg bought it right after their marriage in 1940. They gave it a name by which 4-H projects could be identified. Several years ago, the Sonnenbergs bought a supper club when their son took over the farm. But eventually Lilyan got the farm back, and the land and barn is now rented to a farmer who lives on the property.

"I missed the people in the supper club business," said Lilyan, and the plan was to open a campground. (She camps with a friend in an RV in Florida or other points south every winter.) But neighbors balked, so she opened a B&B instead.

Two guest rooms are in the farmhouse, which was built in 1900 and modernized in 1948. Guests should be aware that in the farmhouse, the tub and shower are downstairs and are shared with the Sonnenbergs. Lilyan shops some estate and antique sales, but furnishings are a mix of old and contemporary.

The farm is 400 acres near the Red Cedar River. Guests can walk in the woods but there are no trails for cross-country skiing. Cows are in the pasture in front of the house, but fraternizing with the animals is not encouraged (they belong to a farmer renting the land). Watch for eagles or deer from the screened porch.

Rooms and Rates: Two - Both upstairs. Yellow room has two twin beds, quilt wall hanging made by Lilyan, modern paneled wall. Blue room has a double bed and another quilt wall hanging. Share half-bath upstairs and tub and shower with owners downstairs. $25 single, $35 double. Add tax.

Meals: Breakfast is served in the farmhouse dining room "whenever you get up." It includes fruit bowl and an entree such as pancakes, omelettes or French toast.

Dates open: April 15-Oct. 15   **Smoking:** Yes

Children: Yes   **Pets:** "Under control"

Nearby: Red Cedar River for canoeing and tubing, 3 miles. Tainter Lake, fishing and boat rentals, supper club, 14 miles. Golf, 10 miles. Eau Claire, 30 miles. Colfax, 7 miles, has sign proclaiming it the half-way point between the Equator and the North Pole.

Location/Directions: Located seven miles north of Colfax on Sunrise Road, off County Road W and Hidden Valley Road. Detailed map sent. Chicago, 8 hours. Madison, 4 hours. Milwaukee, 5.5 hours. Twin Cities, 1.5 hours.

Deposit: None

Payment: Cash, personal or traveler's checks only

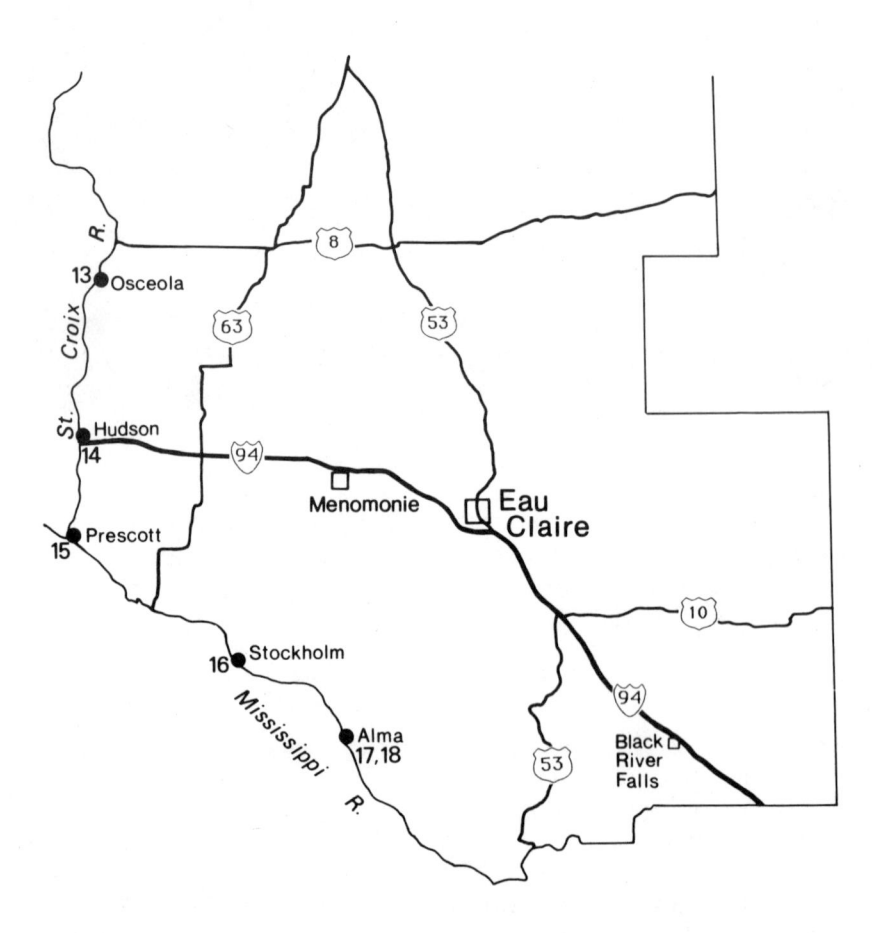

-Indian Head Country - Rivertowns
13. St. Croix River Inn - Osceola.................................... 50-51
14. Jefferson-Day House - Hudson................................ 52-53
15. The Yankee Bugler - Prescott.................................. 54-55
16. Great River Farm - Stockholm................................ 56-57
17. Gallery House - Alma.. 58-59
18. The Laue House - Alma... 60-61

Osceola

St. Croix River Inn
305 River Street
Osceola, WI 54020
715-294-4248

Owner/Operator:
Robert G. Marshall
Innkeeper: Margy Rogers

Robert Marshall, a Minneapolis developer, and his investors are only the second "family" to own this Dutch Colonial building. It was constructed in the early 1900s of stone from a quarry just south of Osceola, then a lumber town making commercial use of the St. Croix River.

The home was built by C.W. and May Staples. Staples was the son of a New Hampshire man who was a miller, merchant and drug store owner in booming Osceola. Staples was born in Illinois in 1852 and moved to Osceola with his parents when he was only 3. He attended local schools and moved to Menominee, Wis., to serve as a bookkeeper, but returned to join his father at the drug store.

May and C.W. Staples had a daughter, Irene, who also became a druggist. For many years, Irene Staples Cooper lived in the stone house overlooking the river. She moved and sold the house to Marshall in 1984.

Marshall's first plans were to turn the thick-walled structure into a condominium on three levels. But he and his architect nixed those plans, and a B&B inn eventually resulted. Extensive renovation involved additions outside the original stone exterior walls, and some of those stone walls are now interior walls.

Suites are named after steamboats built at Osceola and are done in antique reproductions. A game room on the top floor is decorated like a riverboat wheelhouse; a lobby is also for guests' use. Guests find heavy terry robes hanging in the wardrobe. Riverview rooms have either a balcony or patio with chairs, and three have whirlpools at window level for a river view while soaking.

Rooms and Rates: Seven - All with private baths with whirlpools and six with hand-held showers; queen beds. Examples: G.B. Knapp has a four-poster canopy bed, river view sitting room - $150. Maggie Reaney has four-poster bed - $85. Jennie Hays has four-poster canopy bed, huge cathedral riverview windows - $125. Nellie Kent and Minnie Will each have two-poster beds, riverview whirlpools, patios - $100. Osceola Suite is an "apartment" with kitchen, sitting area, dining table - $150. Add tax. Midweek discounts.

Meals: Weekdays, continental breakfast is served to the guest rooms including sweet rolls, muffins and fruit. Hot breakfast on weekends includes quiche.

Dates open: Year 'round

Smoking: Designated areas only

Children: No

Pets: No

Nearby: Shops, restaurants, bars, waterfalls in Osceola, 2-4 blocks. Downhill skiing at two hills, 8-10 minutes. X-c skiing, hiking Interstate State Park or William O'Brien State Park, canoeing St. Croix at Taylor's Falls or tour boats, within 10 minutes.

Location/Directions: In downtown Osceola, turn west on Third Avenue from the main street in town; drive by hospital and church. Inn is on the riverside. Chicago, 8.5 hours. Madison, 5.5 hours. Milwaukee, 7 hours. Twin Cities, 45 minutes.

Deposit: First night's lodging

Payment: Cash, personal or traveler's checks, VISA or MasterCard

Hudson

Jefferson-Day House

1109 Third St.
Hudson, WI 54016
715-386-7111

Owners/Operators:
Sharon and Wally Miller
Marjorie Miller

Albert Harris, a lumberman and a horse fancier, had this huge home built in 1857. But just three years later, when the Civil War heated up, he sold it to Amos Jefferson and headed back to his native South.

Though Jefferson and the subsequent owner, Cecil Day, were both prominent bankers, it is their wives who seem to be long remembered in Hudson history. Mrs. Jefferson was a member of the Ladies Literary Society, and her house became their 500-volume library. During the Civil War, members subscribed to periodicals to scan the "missing in action" lists. The Days bought the home in 1919. Genevieve Day was a historian who wrote "Hudson in the Early Days," an account of the lumbertown's beginnings, which is still on sale in a downtown bookstore.

Over the next half-century, the house changed owners and was changed itself. The biggest change was about 50 years ago, when half of it was severed and moved to the next block, becoming a separate house (the main house is so big, it's hard to picture it any bigger). It's easy to imagine the Literary Society members descending the winding staircase or walking down the long halls -- doorways are still wide enough for hoop skirts. Rewiring, papering, painting, new ceilings and plumbing were needed, however, before the B&B opened in December 1986.

Sharon and Wally Miller joke that they needed to buy this beauty in order to store the antiques they collected. (That's not far from truth, since they did have almost all the furniture needed.) Both teachers, they have a variety of interests, including traveling in B&Bs, boating the St. Croix and hunting antiques for their antique business. Those interests were perfect for starting a B&B. With Wally's mother, Marjorie, willing and eager to live in the house, and daughter Angie as the summer breakfast server, the Millers all are involved in the family business.

Guests have appetizers and soft drinks in the evening, and are welcome to use the library's fireplace and games, the living and dining rooms and front porch swing. Guests arriving by boat will be picked up at the marina, and honeymoon and anniversary couples receive complimentary champagne or a box of chocolates.

Meals: Breakfast is served in the dining room at 9:30 or a time arranged the night before. It may include brandied strawberries with cream, hot orange poppyseed muffins with cream cheese butter, baked ham and egg crepes, and individual cherry cheesecakes for dessert. Entrees vary and may be pannekoekens or egg strudel.

Rooms and Rates: Four - All upstairs, carpeted, furnished in antiques with window air conditioners. St. Croix Suite has three rooms, antique double bed and brass trundle bed on sun porch, private bath with tub and shower - $80 doubles, $110 for three or four persons. Captain's Room has brass bed, done in navy and white, private bath with shower only - $65. Harbor Room has lace curtains, antiques and stenciling - $45. Hudson Room has four-poster bed, wicker furniture and antique doll collection, done in blue and white - $55. Harbor and Hudson Rooms share bath with tub and shower. Rates are singles or doubles. Add tax.

Dates open: Weekends, year 'round; weekdays June - August

Smoking: Not in guest rooms   **Children:** Over 9   **Pets:** No

Nearby: Octagon House tours, 1 block. Downtown shops and restaurants, 4 blocks. Phipps Center for the Arts, 5 blocks. St. Croix River beach, boat launch, park, 7 blocks. Downhill skiing at Afton Alps or Welch Village, x-c skiing at William O'Brien State Park, 7 miles. Bike trail, 1 mile. Tubing down Apple River, Somerset, 10 miles.

Location/Directions: From I-94, take exit into downtown. Turn right on Myrtle, turn left on Third, house is on the left in the middle of the block. Detailed map sent. Chicago, 8 hours. Madison, 5 hours. Milwaukee, 6.5 hours. Twin Cities, half-hour.

Deposit: Half of room rate

Payment: Cash, personal or traveler's checks only

Prescott

The Yankee Bugler
506 Oak St.
Prescott, WI 54021
715-262-3019

Owners/Operators:
Mari and Mark Otterson

The first hint of what's to come at this B&B is the doorbell. The 1879 bell, original to the house, does not resemble today's electronic gadgets in the least.

The second hint is when Mari Otterson opens the door. She's dressed in a white apron and cap over a long skirt. Guests are ushered into the parlor and soon offered Lee's Lime Pie (yes, named after the General) and a tall glass of lemonade.

The historic detail with which this B&B has been done will not be forgotten for a moment during the stay. There are antique shaving soap and cough drop boxes hidden in the medicine cabinet, antique dominoes and checkers in the parlor, and antique alarm clocks at bedside. Some time during the stay, Mark Otterson will appear with hat, arm bands and bow tie. Breakfast is served by Mark and Mari's niece, dressed as a Victorian school girl.

All this fun (and they *are* having fun) is in honor of the Yankee Bugler, George Nichols, who was wounded in the Civil War as the chief bugler for Wisconsin's Second Calvary. Nichols or his descendents owned the house, built in 1854, from 1860 to 1942. For years, he had a music school in the parlor, an office in a side room, and a factory in a back room, where he and two carpenters built melodians (forerunners of the pump organ) and pianos.

Mari and Mark bought this home when it was being sold off as one of several cottages to a hospital. They spent two-and-a-half years restoring it before opening in July 1987. In Mari's words, "If you can touch it, we did it." Mari is a commercial artist who became familiar with historic B&Bs when doing art for the Minnesota Historic B&B Association, headquartered in nearby Hastings.

Guests may use the parlor, porch, second floor library and the patio, and are treated to homemade truffles before bed, as well as a welcoming dessert. Firewood and marshmallows are provided for use of the campfire pit in the backyard.

Rooms and Rates: Three - All suites. The Yankee's Rose - Antique brass bed, black walnut rocker, canopied bath with tub only, done in red velvet and pink roses - $69. Alabama's Fancy - Four-poster canopy bed, canopied single bed, window seat that can sleep a child, lace curtains, bath with clawfoot tub with shower - $79. The Bugler's Serenade - Pre-Civil War four-poster bed, sitting and dressing rooms, done in dusty rose and antique lace - $89. Rates are doubles; singles $5 less. Each additional person, $5. Add tax.

Meals: Breakfast is served in the dining room or to the rooms 8-10, and guests are summoned to the table by music played on the Victrola. It may include Southern peaches in a fruit bowl with whipped cream, Mason-Dixon apple-raisin Muffins, Blue Coat Egg Bundles (baked eggs, ham and pimento), and Hurry Scurry Fat Back (bacon). Two kinds of muffins are usually baked and served with homemade apple or honey butter.

Dates open: Year 'round   **Smoking:** Yes

Children: Over 10   **Pets:** No

Nearby: Downtown restaurants and shops, 4 blocks. Marinas, excursion boats, 5 blocks. Prescott Beach (swimming in St. Croix River), 4 blocks. Vinyards and wineries, 6 miles. Afton State Park (hiking, beach, x-c skiing), downhill skiing at Welch Village or Afton Alps, 5 miles. Carpenter Nature Center (x-c skiing, hiking, programs), 2.5 miles.

Location/Directions: In downtown Prescott, go straight up the hill on Cherry, the same street the bridge is on. In four blocks, turn left on Court, then right on Oak. Inn is on the left. Chicago, 8 hours. Madison, 4.5 hours. Milwaukee, 6.5 hours. Twin Cities, half-hour.

Deposit: First night's lodging

Payment: Cash, personal or traveler's checks, or AMEX

Stockholm

Great River Farm

General Delivery
Stockholm, WI 54769
715-442-5656

Owner/Operator:
Leland P. Krebs, Jr.

The Peterson family founded Stockholm, which overlooks the Mississippi River's Lake Pepin, in 1854, and brother Jacob built this stone house on the southern edge of town in 1869. Three generations of Petersons lived on the farm until Leland Krebs bought it in 1980.

Krebs, who lived in St. Paul and then Florida, "came back specifically to sheep farm. I was just acting on a dream of mine to have a small farm," he said. For four years, until 1984, he actively farmed the 45 acres, then reached a point with the economics of the business where he had to expand or leave sheep farming. He chose not to expand, and opened a B&B in late 1984 after rewiring, replumbing, scraping and painting. "I wanted a way to make the property productive in some way." Crops now cover 20 acres, and guests are free to roam over the land.

Structurally, no changes had been made in the house. The first floor is built into the hillside. Heated by wood, guests can sit around the parlor woodstove. Blair & Ketchum's "Country Journal" sits alongside the binoculars for viewing the migratory birds using the Mississippi flyway.

"Guests have pretty much the feel of visiting a friend here," Krebs said. "It's a restful, scenic and serene environment." Some come specifically to eat at the renowned Harbor View Cafe in Pepin, where Krebs works as a bartender; he checks people in, shows them around and then they have the place to themselves. Breakfast is whenever guests like, sometimes served on the porch, and Krebs is available all morning.

Rooms and Rates: Two - Both with double beds, down comforters, original wood floors, family antiques and period pieces. Both share bath with tub and shower. One room is $45, other one a larger room with huge wooden bed and working woodstove - $55. Singles $5 less; no extra person.

Meals: Breakfast is served at guests' leisure and may include fresh fruit, fresh eggs, French toast, waffles; homemade muffins, gingerbread or coffeecake; fresh ground coffee.

Dates open: March 1 through November   **Smoking:** On porch only

Children: Depends - check with owner   **Pets:** No

Nearby: Lake Pepin on Mississippi and Stockholm, 2 blocks, with art gallery with local artists, country store, rare and used book shop, and Amish country store. Marina and restaurant in Pepin, 6 miles. Birdwatching, sailing, hiking, bicycling.

Location/Directions: Stockholm is on Highway 35 along Mississippi. The farm is also on 35, with the red barn and farm buildings at south edge of Stockholm. Chicago, 6.5 hours. Madison, 4 hours. Milwaukee, 5.5 hours. Twin Cities, 1 hour.

Deposit: $25 per night reserved

Payment: Cash, personal or traveler's checks only

Alma

Gallery House
215 N. Main
Alma, WI 54610
608-685-4975

Owners/Operators:
Joan and John Runions

This three-room B&B is located in an historic mercantile building whose first floor has served Alma since 1861 as restaurants, a hardware store, post office, library, floor covering store, antique shops and dentist offices.

Jacob Iberg had the building constructed for a store and home. Peter Polin and John Tester leased and then owned the building from the 1860s, operating a general store that did an excellent business as Alma grew as a grain depot. The Polin family remained owners until 1913.

Today, the building is on the National Register of Historic Places. John Runions' watercolor studio is located there along with a gallery. Joan Runions operates the Gallery Spice Shoppe on the other side of the gallery. Runions moved in 1974 from Chicago with two of their four children for John's business.

"The scenery is the biggest thing," he said. "The material is here." When they drove through Alma and the area, "Lake Pepin just rang bells." The store was empty then, and the family lived upstairs. After the youngest children moved out, "we had all this space," Joan said. They opened the B&B in June 1985, after replumbing, rewiring and redecorating.

The B&B is upstairs in what used to be, at various times, a boarding house and apartments. Guests enter the long hall from the back, and they have access to the Runions' living and dining rooms at the end of the hall. The three rooms are off the hall and share a bath. A deck goes around the side of the building for guests' use.

Rooms and Rates: Three - All doubles, share bath with clawfoot tub and shower. One has a sink in the room and all are done in yellow and gold. Brass bed in #3, antique wood bed in #2. $35 per room. Add tax.

Meals: Breakfast is served in the dining room at 8 (so the shops can open at 9) and includes fresh fruit plate or compote, homemade raisin bran muffins, cheese and sausage fritatta, pancakes or French toast, bacon.

Dates open: Year 'round **Smoking:** No

Children: No **Pets:** No

Nearby: Country roads for fall colors; river fishing. Lock and dam, 1 block. Trail up to Buena Vista Park, overlooks Mississippi, in back of house. Swimming beach, canoe rental, tennis court, marina with boat rental, 1 mile. Golf, 8 miles south.

Location/Directions: Alma is on Highway 35 along the Mississippi. Gallery House is downtown. Chicago, 6 hours. Madison, 3.5 hours. Milwaukee, 5 hours. Twin Cities, 1.5 hours.

Deposit: First night's lodging

Payment: Cash, personal or traveler's checks, VISA or MasterCard

Alma

The Laue House

1111 S. Main
Alma, WI 54610
608-685-4923

Owners/Operators:
Jan and Jerry Schreiber

Jan and Jerry Schreiber, who are natives of nearby Nelson, Wis., and Alma, respectively, are retired and enjoy restoring historic buildings. The Laue House was built in 1863 by successful sawmill owner Fred Laue, a German immigrant who moved to Alma after living in Cincinnati. It is on the National Register of Historic Places.

When the Schreibers bought the single-family home overlooking the Mississippi in 1977, only three rooms on the first floor were being used. It had no eaves, light fixtures or furniture, and the porch was falling off. Schreibers found the original architectural drawings in the attic, from which they had decorative wrought iron and 27 wooden brackets replicated.

"My original intention was to save this domestic Italianate structure, being as it's the only one in Alma," said Jerry. But when a power plant was constructed nearby and workers wanted to rent rooms, the idea for a B&B was conceived.

This place is spartan and casual. If Jan and Jerry aren't in, guests check themselves in and pick an empty room. Likewise, breakfast is toast-your-own English muffin. Guests may use the player piano downstairs and a refrigerator. Don't expect little individual bars of soap and matching towels; guests share a bar of soap just like at home, the upstairs bathroom shower stall is utilitarian, and rooms are not carpeted.

Schreibers will take guests on parties on river sandbars, and they rent canoes and provide shuttle service. Guests can clean fish or cook out in the back. The front porch is a favorite spot to sit and watch the river go by. Trains speed by and rattle the windows.

Rooms and Rates: Five - All upstairs. The large white room overlooks the river, has two double beds, plus a small color cable TV and a sink - $18 single, $28. The other rooms have B&W cable TV - $15 single, $24 double. All share a bath with a shower. A tub is available downstairs. Add tax.

Meals: Breakfast is serve-yourself English muffin, grape jelly and coffee.

Dates open: Usually closed January - March, but call ahead.

Smoking: Yes   **Children:** "Small families are OK"

Pets: "We love pets if they're well-behaved." Schreibers have a dog.

Nearby: Country roads for fall colors. River fishing. Lock and dam within walking distance. Boat rental across the highway, Schriebers rent canoes. Free boat launching. Swimming, tennis. Golf, 8 miles.

Location/Directions: Alma is on Highway 35 along the Mississippi. Laue House is last house on south side of town, near power plant. Chicago, 6 hours. Madison, 3.5 hours. Milwaukee, 5 hours. Twin Cities, 1.5 hours.

Deposit: Not necessary

Payment: Cash, personal or traveler's checks only

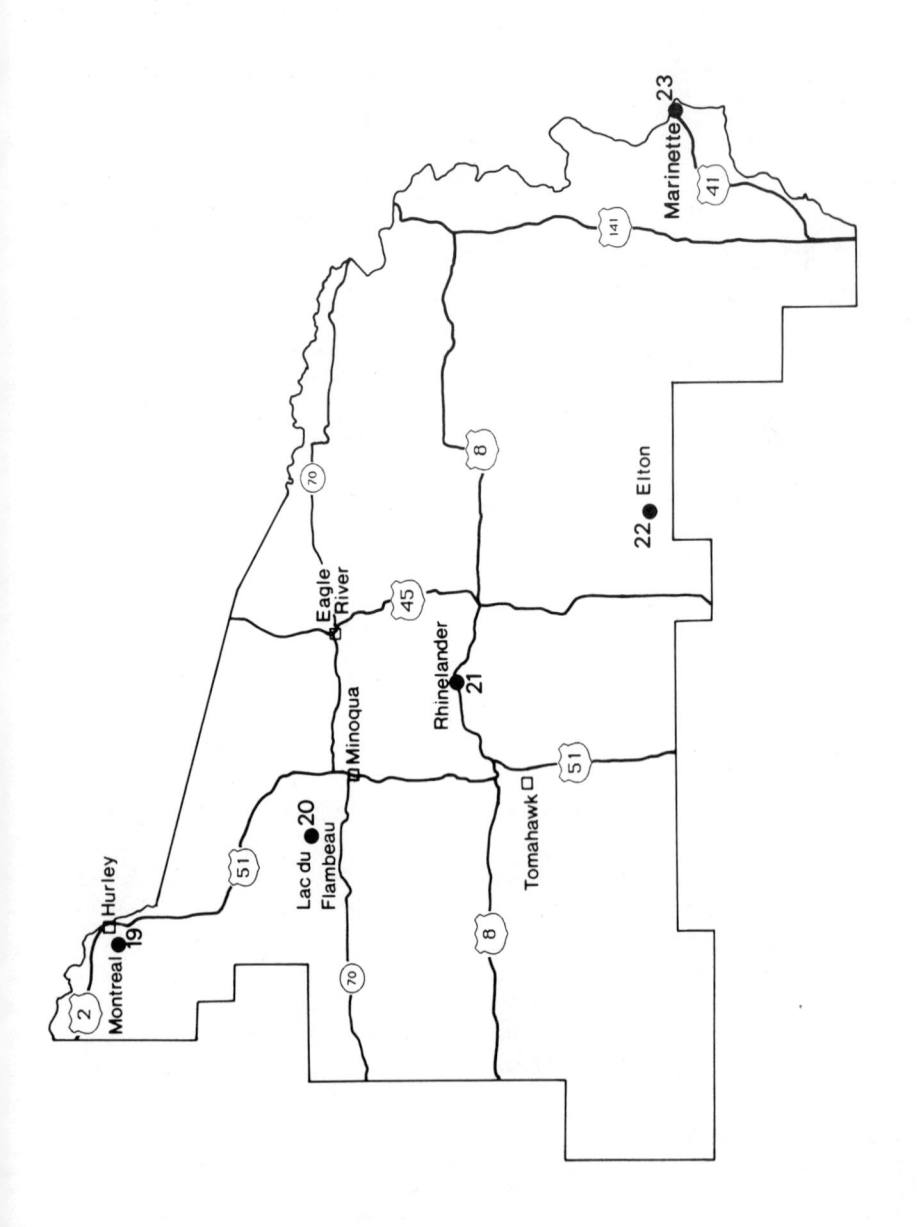

-Northwoods
19. The Inn - Montreal..64-65
20. Chippewa Lodge B&B - Lac du Flambeau......................66-67
21. Cranberry Hill B&B Inn - Rhinelander.......................... 68-69
22. Glacier Wilderness B&B - Elton....................................70-71
23. Lauerman Guest House Inn - Marinette........................ 72-73

Montreal

The Inn

Wisconsin Avenue
Montreal, WI 54550
715-561-5180
414-233-1505 - Schumachers in Oshkosh

Owners/Operators:
Dick and Doree Schumacher
Jim Schumacher, son

Montreal was a company town, where the Oglebay-Norton iron mining company built houses, planted gardens and made each corner lot a playground for its employees and their families. The 700 men once employed by the mine worked underneath the town in what is said to be the largest underground iron mine in the U.S., with a shaft reaching 4,337 feet down. Before the mine closed in 1963, nearly 46 million tons of ore had come from the Montreal Mine. The town is now on the National Register of Historic Places.

The miners (or, more often, their wives) used to line up each week to collect a paycheck at the office headquarters. That building is now The Inn. Built in 1913, the building housed the mine superintendent's office on the first floor, along with three secretaries and a waiting room. The second floor was the engineering department, and the third floor had labs for the chemistry department. The thick concrete vault, which held the precious payroll and the mine's core samples, stretches from the basement to the third floor.

For a time, the building was part of the Iron Gate Inn with six kitchenette apartments for rent. Then Doree and Dick Schumacher, both teachers in Oshkosh, and their two sons, all avid skiers, found themselves in the area every winter weekend. They purchased a small house in the neighborhood and, later, several others, which they rented to skiers. Meanwhile, for several years, the office building stood vacant. Everytime the Schumachers drove by, Doree would say, "Someone should do something with that lovely old building."

So they did. For five years, they operated a private alpine ski school in it, where potential world-class teens studied and skied. Since their plans were to retire to the area and since they enjoy people, they redid the building as a B&B in 1982. Many antiques in the Inn are family heirlooms. Guests may use the living, dining and TV rooms downstairs. In the winter, an apres' ski hour by the fireplace includes hors d'oeuvres and beverages, and gives guests a chance to visit.

Meals: Breakfast is served in the dining room at a time arranged the night before. In the summer, it may include scrambled eggs, toast, wild fruit jelly, and homemade applesauce, or cottage cheese pancakes and fresh fruit. In the winter, it may be Belgian waffles, eggs, fried potatoes and sausage.

Rooms and Rates: Three - All upstairs suites with at least two double beds in separate bedrooms, carpeted, with private baths with tub and shower. #1 has one antique double bed and second bed has crocheted bedspread. #2 has two double beds, one a spool bed. #3 has two bedrooms with double beds plus a third floor loft with six twin beds and an extra bath with shower only. $35 single, $75 double, winter; $20 single, $40 double, summer. Each additional person, $15. Add tax.

Dates open: Year 'round   **Smoking:** Not encouraged

Children: "Well-behaved children welcomed"   **Pets:** "By arrangement"

Nearby: Downhill skiing at Big Powderhorn, BlackJack, IndianHead and WhiteCap mountains, within 20 minutes. X-c skiing, out the door; 20K groomed trail system connects nearby. Beach and fishing, 3 miles. Copper Falls State Park, 15 miles. Porcupine Mountains State Park, 30 miles. Ski flying.

Location/Directions: Take Highway 51 north to Highway 77, then west 3 miles. Hwy. 77 becomes Wisconsin Avenue in Montreal, and Inn is on the north side. Chicago, 8 hours. Madison, 6 hours. Milwaukee, 6.5 hours. Twin Cities, 4.5 hours.

Deposit: Half of room rate; full amount for one night stays

Payment: Cash, personal or traveler's checks only

Lac du Flambeau

Chippewa Lodge B&B

3525 Chippewa Lodge Trail
Lac du Flambeau, WI 54538
715-588-3297
September-May: P.O. Box 22388
Honolulu, HI 96816
808-734-7159

Owners/Operators:
Ann Rayson and Ben Bess

"An outdoor retreat for the whole family...friendly, clean-cut clientele...food better than good...swimming, hiking, scenic drives, Indian pageants" --
1920s brochure, Dormeyer's Chippewa Lodge

Ann Rayson and Ben Bess have had little to rewrite for their B&B brochure, since all of the above is still true. And the Lodge remains the only commercial operation on Ike Walton Lake, whose 12 miles of shoreline is mostly undeveloped. But these are people with senses of humor, and they chose to add the lodge is "*a charming blend of Fawlty Towers, Bob Newhart's Lodge and Lake Wobegon.*"

The Lodge, open 10 weeks in the summer, is bare-foot casual. Everyone swims off the dock out in front, including a family of mallards. A ping-pong table is set up in the dining room and popcorn is served before bedtime. Bait is stored in the old cola machine in the kitchen, and the lures and postcards that came with the place still are on display.

Another addition to the brochure was mileage to Lac du Flambeau from Hawaii (5,000). Ann grew up in the Chicago area, but spent summers at her parents' cabin near here. After she and Ben moved to Hawaii, they continued to return (Ann is an English professor at the University of Hawaii; Ben's Bess Press publishes regional books, many of which are produced on a school-year schedule).

In the summer of 1983, they saw the Lodge was for sale. They looked at the place, closed the next day and were on a plane home to Hawaii the day after that. There's space here their three children can't have in Hawaii, and the B&B is both business and pleasure for Ann and Ben. Plumbing and sagging ceilings were re-done and rooms redecorated, and the B&B opened in 1987. Guests can use the rowboat and bicycles, hear the loons and bullfrogs at night and watch the stars from the dock. On cool nights there is a fire in the fieldstone fireplace.

Rooms and Rates: Four - All upstairs, with sink in each room, knotty pine chair rails and some country wallpaper. Two half-baths and one tub and shower down the hall. Guests choose rooms by proximity to lake or firmness of mattresses. Rooms 2, 3 and 4 have double beds; Room 1 has two twins. $25 single, $35 double. Add tax.

Meals: Breakfast is served in the dining room 8-9 or at a time arranged the night before. It may include eggs, omelettes, quiche, fresh wild berry pancakes or waffles, bacon or sausage, homemade banana bread or English muffins, and Kona coffee from Hawaii.

Dates open: Early June - Late August   **Smoking:** On porch only

Children: Yes   **Pets:** No

Nearby: Swimming and fishing in the lake. Motor rentals, 3 miles. Sea plane rides may be arranged on the lake. Restaurants, 3-10 miles. Fish hatcheries, tribal bingo, Indian pow-wows in Lac du Flambeau, 5 miles. Golf and tennis, 5 miles. Horseback riding and attractions in Woodruff-Minocqua, 10 miles. Berry picking, hiking, biking from the Lodge; bike trails in area.

Location/Directions: From Highways 51 or 47, take County Road H to Chippewa Lodge sign (3 miles from 47, 5 miles from 51). Chicago, 7 hours. Madison, 4 hours. Milwaukee, 5.5 hours. Twin Cities, 5 hours.

Deposit: First night's lodging

Payment: Cash, personal or traveler's checks only

Rhinelander

Cranberry Hill B&B Inn

209 E. Frederick St.
Rhinelander, WI 54501
715-369-3504

Owners/Operators:
Karen Hodges Minassi
and family

In 1894, an architect from New York was called in to design this English Renaissance home for the wife of one of Rhinelander's most successful businessmen. Over the years, Edward O. Brown was president of Brown Lumber Co., the Rhinelander Paper Mill, the first refrigeration company in town and a local bank, sometimes going into partnership with his brothers Anderson and Webster.

He and Clara, his wife, raised five surviving children in the huge house. The Browns were well-liked in the community, and they both died in 1935. Another president of Rhinelander Paper Mill, Folke Becker, owned the house after the Browns. Alice Becker, his wife, stayed in the house until her death in 1973.

Three others had owned the house before Karen Hodges Minassi found it languishing on the market. As a single family home, it was too big and too hard to heat for most families. Minassi was living near San Francisco, and she came back to Rhinelander each year, as she had as a child, to a family summer home.

"I was familiar with B&Bs there (in San Francisco) and I felt this would make an excellent B&B with the large public spaces and more private bedrooms. It was large enough to feel more like a small hotel." She found it in excellent condition, requiring only wallpapering, painting and furnishing. The woodwork had never been painted and the mechanical systems already had been updated. The overgrown grounds were trimmed back, and in 1982 the B&B opened for summer business only.

Since 1985, Cranberry Hill has been open year 'round. Guests may use the parlor, living room (fires are lit in both in the winter), sun porch and dining room.

Rooms and Rates: Eight - Examples include: Raspberry Room on first floor has white iron double bed, private bath with shower only, marble sink - $65. Can be rented with parlor and living room as a suite - $75. On second floor: Master Bedroom has double brass bed, done in blues - $65. It shares bath (shower only) with Family Bedroom, the former ballroom with a king, two twins and crib - $75. Pink Room has white iron bed, garden view, hardwood floors - $55. It shares bath (shower only) with Side Porch, one twin bed, white eyelet curtains - $45. No charge for additional person in the room. Add tax.

Meals: Breakfast served buffet-style on the porch or in front of fire at 9. It may include coffeecakes, rolls or croissants, jams, cheeses and fruit, or broccoli, tomato and onion quiche, baked goods and fruit, or French toast and bacon.

Dates open: Year 'round   **Smoking:** Yes

Children: Yes   **Pets:** Yes

Nearby: Downtown restaurants and shops, 2 blocks. Rhinelander Logging Museum, half-mile. Fishing, swimming and boating, 2-5 miles. X-c skiing, 5 miles.

Location/Directions: Go through downtown Rhinelander. Frederick Street is at the last block of downtown. Turn right to the inn, which is on the left (sign posted). Chicago, 6.5 hours. Madison, 4 hours. Milwaukee, 4.5 hours. Twin Cities, 4 hours.

Deposit: $25

Payment: Cash, personal or traveler's checks only

Elton

Glacier Wilderness B&B

Box 12
Elton, WI 54430
715-882-5262

Owners/Operators:
Raeburn and Emil DeHart

Today, Elton does not appear to be much more than a sign on Highway 64. But 100 years ago, this was a bustling community where the Chicago Northwestern Railroad shipped out the lumber from the Crocker Chair Company sawmill to its factories. The railroad spurred off the Soo Line route by White Lake and ran into Antigo. This B&B was the section house, about 100 years old and home to foremen responsible for the tracks, the last of whom was John Kondzela.

"He lived here when I was a child," said Raeburn DeHart, who now owns the section house with her husband, Emil. DeHarts have owned the house twice, once more than 20 years ago when they thought her health was failing. As the state's second blood relative kidney transplant patient, she regained her health and they bought the house back for a summer home in 1956, "one month before the last train went through." Now they live there year 'round.

DeHarts and Linda and Mick West, across the highway, both opened B&Bs as part of their Glacier Wilderness Tours business. (Linda and Mick have a new log cabin home.) Their tour company provides narrated horse-drawn tours of the Crocker Chair Company's logging roads. In the summer, the Belgians pull straw-filled wagons. In the winter, they pull the same bobsleds that lumberjacks used to pull the logs from the woods. Raeburn has plenty of first-hand knowledge to share with guests. Her father was a lumberjack who sawed logs with the infamous cross-cut saw, lived in bunkhouses and was away for weeks at a time.

As the tour business grew (it started in 1982), "a lot of people expressed a desire to stay overnight," she said. Since they opened the house as a B&B in 1987, "we've entertained people from several foreign countries and almost every state...I tell guests this is like Grandma and Grandpa's house. We're very informal."

Guests can watch the mallard ducks in the pond from the dining room, walk down to the barn to see the horses, or fish in the trout stream that runs through the property. When sap runs in maple trees, they can watch syrup-making.

Rooms and Rates: Two - Both on second floor with some modern decor. One room has two double beds, electric fireplace, paneled with gold bedspreads. Other room has double antique white iron bed, wicker rocker, done in beige and gold. Bathroom is downstairs with tub and shower, shared with the hosts. $35 single or double. Each additional person, $10. Add tax.

Meals: Breakfast is served at a time arranged the night before in the dining room facing the woods and duck pond. It may include pancakes with maple syrup made by DeHarts from their trees, ham or sausage, eggs any style and hot biscuits.

Dates open: Year 'round   **Smoking:** Yes

Children: Yes   **Pets:** Not encouraged

Nearby: Trout stream on property. Wagon/sleigh tours with campfire meals available. Trout ponds and deer park, 1 block. Wolf River rafting booked by Wests and DeHarts, 3 miles. X-c skiing on ungroomed trails, across the street; groomed trails, 10 miles. Restaurants, movies and museum in Antigo, 13 miles. Downhill skiing, 30 miles.

Location/Directions: Look for sign on highway at Elton. West's log cabin B&B and sign for the tours is on the right, DeHart's is on the left down the next road past West's driveway (turn in and drive slowly in case the ducks are loose). Chicago, 5.5 hours. Madison, 5 hours. Milwaukee, 4 hours. Twin Cities, 5.5 hours.

Deposit: $20 per couple

Payment: Cash, personal or traveler's checks, or MasterCard

Marinette

Lauerman Guest House Inn

1975 Riverside Ave.
Marinette, WI 54143
715-732-4407

Owners:
    Doris and Leonard Spaude
Operators:
    Sherry and Steve Homa

Black walnut, mahogany, oak and birdseye maple, leaded glass and intricate mouldings were all used in this mansion on the Menominee River. Built for Joseph Lauerman over four years, the home was finished in 1910, costing $17,500.

Lauerman was not always so well to do. In the late 1800s, the young Lauerman worked as a clerk in the Jacob Bremmer General Store, serving lumbermen and pioneers in northeastern Wisconsin and the southwestern Upper Peninsula. When he saved $1,000, he went into business with his brothers.

The Lauerman Brothers Co. moved into a three-story building in downtown Marinette in 1904, where it continued doing business until 1987. By 1920, sales were $5 million a year. Eventually, the company had 39 stores and owned Marinette Knitting Mills, with New York, Chicago and Los Angeles offices.

Joseph and Cecilia Lauerman entertained at their estate until Joseph died in the early 1920s. Cecilia lived here until her death. Their son, Henry and his wife, Ruth, then lived in the home. After Ruth's death in 1984, the Spaudes, and their daughter and son-in-law purchased the home in 1985.

"My husband and I have been in the hotel business all of our lives," said Sherry, who met Steve when they worked at the Holiday Inn, four blocks away. They wanted to open their own inn and restaurant, serving three meals a day and of sufficient style and quality to warrant a dress code and carriage rides on Sundays.

Original light fixtures and leaded glass remain downstairs, as does the handpainted mural in the dining room, and woodwork remains throughout. Rotted walls were replaced, new carpeting, plumbing and wiring was put in, five baths were added and two were redone. Two bedrooms and a dining room were added. Sherry and Steve also own a landscaping company, so they spent four weeks getting debris out of the yard and beginning to redo it. The guest rooms opened in November 1986. Plans call for the restaurant to be in the living room, parlor and music room, with informal dining in the cellar.

Rooms and Rates: Seven - All upstairs with private baths, some with river view. Examples include Cecilia's Room, with original birdseye maple woodwork and fireplace, double brass bed, TV, bath with soaking tub and shower. Lincoln and Freda's rooms have single whirlpools. $50 single, $58 double. Each additional person, $10. Add tax.

Meals: Breakfast is served in the dining room from 7-10:30 and is ordered from the menu. Lunch and dinner are open to the public.

Dates open: Year 'round

Smoking: Yes

Children: Over 14

Pets: No

Nearby: Fishing in the Menominee River, across the street on the railroad bridge. Marina, 2 blocks. Downtown Marinette, 3 blocks. Stephenson Island Logging Museum, 4 blocks.

Location/Directions: From Highway 61, go through town to last corner with stoplight before going over the river. Turn left on Riverside Avenue; inn is on left in about three blocks. Chicago, 6 hours. Madison, 4 hours. Milwaukee, 3.5 hours. Twin Cities, 6 hours.

Deposit: Full amount

Payment: Cash, personal or traveler's checks, VISA or MasterCard

32 ●Wausau

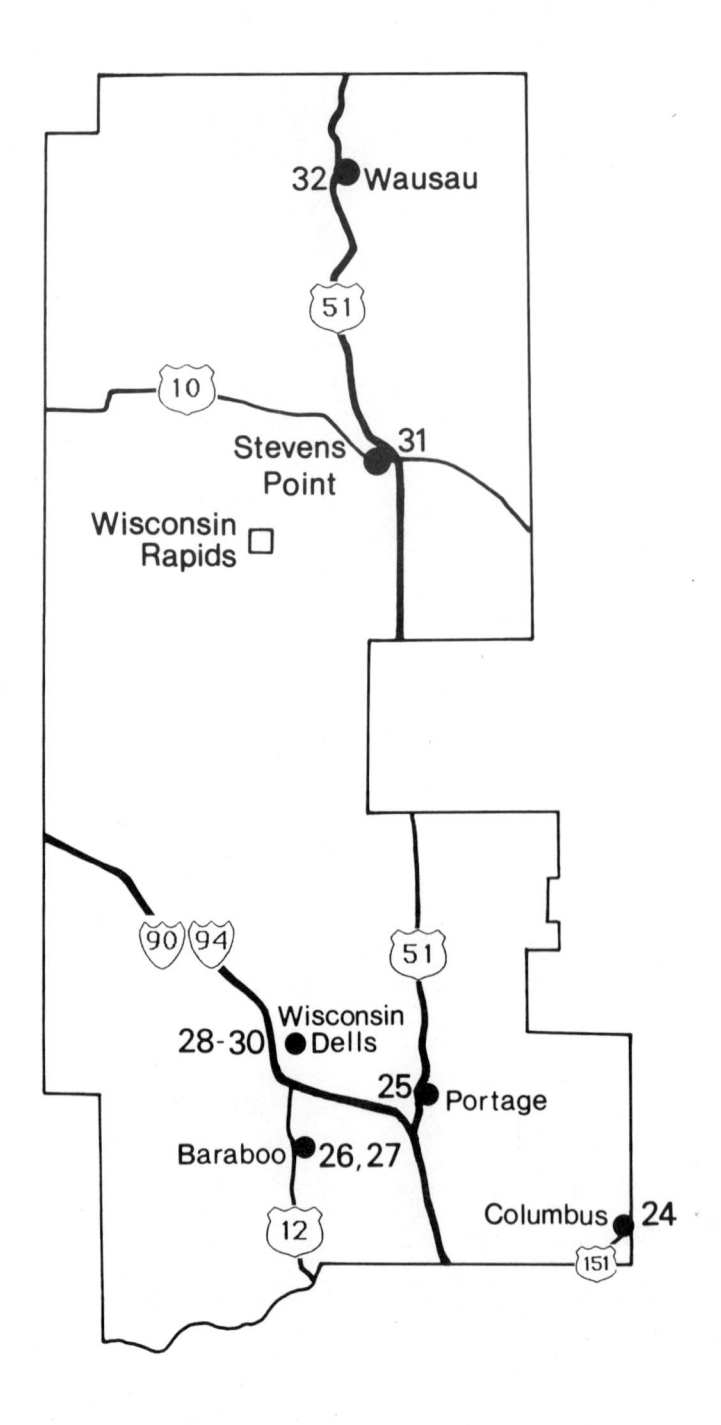

(51)

(10)

Stevens
●31
Point

Wisconsin □
Rapids

(90)(94)

(51)

28-30 ●Wisconsin
       Dells
          ●25 ●Portage

Baraboo●●26,27

(12)

Columbus● 24
(151)

-Central Wisconsin River Country

24. By the Okeag Guest House - Columbus............................ 76-77
25. Bonnie Oaks Estate - Portage... 78-79
26. The Barrister's House - Baraboo..................................... 80-81
27. House of Seven Gables - Baraboo....................................82-83
28. B&B House on River Road - Wisconsin Dells................... 84-85
29. Historic Bennett House - Wisconsin Dells........................ 86-87
30. Sherman House - Wisconsin Dells.................................. 88-89
31. The Victorian Swan on Water - Stevens Point................... 90-91
32. Rosenberry Inn - Wausau...92-93

Columbus

By the Okeag Guest House

446 Wisconsin St.
Columbus, WI 53965
414-623-3007

Owners/Operators:
Bernetta and Alton Mather

You'd never know to look at it, but this little riverside guest house was once a small horse barn.

Standing inside, watching the river go by, Alton Mather points to where the hay chute and the manger were, right about where the sliding glass door was installed and the comfortable reading chair now sits.

As near as the Mathers can tell, the home was built about 1911. The owner, Emma Klatt, owned property along the riverbank near downtown Columbus. She sold fruit and vegetables, and either the garden or her mode of transportation, or both, required the use of a horse.

Mathers bought the property in 1979 with no intention of going into the hospitality business. "I like old houses," said Bernetta. "We owned an old brick house (to retire to). We had farmed all our lives and had remodeled several houses. We decided we'd buy this, remodel it and sell or rent it."

At the time, "it was so overgrown you couldn't even see the river," which flows slowly by about 50 feet from the guest house. "We had it all cleared and fell in love with the river," she said. Pictures they have of the house when they bought it show a rather ordinary and slightly run-down house. The "after" photo, and in-person results, are stunning; the house now is a Victorian beauty.

The horse barn was used for garage and storage, but the dirt-floored structure was converted to a guest house for their children, who had no place to stay in the one-bedroom main house. The original barn is now the living area, done in country decor, and a loft-like bedroom was added. It opened the summer of 1986.

A Wisconsin cheese tray, with fruit and crackers, awaits guests. The river has a slow current and can be canoed 3-4 miles upstream. The yard has a hammock and the guest house has a brick patio.

Rooms and Rates: One - a furnished guest house. Downstairs, living area has sofa hide-a-bed and chairs, TV; kitchenette comes furnished (even a microwave) and stocked with breakfast items. Bath has shower only. Upstairs, two twin trundle beds can fold out to make four twins. A window air conditioner is installed in the upstairs bedroom; the room is carpeted and decorated with family heirlooms and antique toys. $50 single. Each additional person, $5. Add tax. Senior citizen cash discount of 10 percent.

Meals: Fix-your-own. Refrigerator and kitchen comes stocked with wine, cheese, butter, English muffins, coffee and juice. Furnished kitchenette has microwave and linens, etc.

Dates open: Year 'round   **Smoking:** No

Children: Over 9   **Pets:** No

Nearby: Pier with canoe and paddleboat. Biking route map provided to guests. Antique mall in Columbus (said to be largest in Wisconsin with 92 dealers), 1 mile. Dodge County Park (camping, picnicking, nature trails), 3 miles. Farmer's market in Madison on Saturdays, half-hour. Wisconsin Dells, 1 hour.

Location/Directions: From Highway 16/James Street intersects Lewis Street. Turn northeast on Lewis, go one block to Wisconsin Street, turn south. Guest house is at end of street on left behind the gray-and-white main house. Chicago, 3 hours. Madison, half-hour. Milwaukee, 1.5 hours. Twin Cities, 5.5 hours.

Deposit: First night's lodging

Payment: Cash, personal or traveler's checks, VISA or MasterCard

Portage

Bonnie Oaks Estate

Rural Route 3, Box 147
Portage, WI 53901
608-981-2057

Owner/Operator:
Bill Schultz

Guests who turn off the country road to Bonnie Oaks will be surprised anything so secluded, so serene, so well-kept and so historic could be so close to the Wisconsin Dells. This 80-acre estate, listed as a National Historic District, has guest houses restored to the state in which summer guests enjoyed them in the 1880s -- plus modern plumbing.

Cyrus Woodman first claimed this acreage in 1853, selling it a year later for $100 to John Breatcliffe. He lived upstairs in a log building; the sheep lived downstairs (now it's home to tractors and tools). In 1857, a man from Vermont, Joshua Atwood, paid $725 for the property, bringing grape vines from his home state. Atwoods' daughter, Alma, named it Bonnie Oaks. She married John Ormsby, an inventor who built a windmill to power an early version of an underground sprinkler system.

Their daughter, Mildred Green, was yesteryear's version of a party girl. She drew friends from all over who came to enjoy the estate in the summer. Russian pianist Josef Lhevinne came for 20 summers from New York, each time bringing his disassembled grand piano, reassembling it in the Tower House (formerly the windmill). Paul Robeson, the famous baritone and actor in " Ol' Man River," also was a frequent guest, as were Pulitzer-prize winning playwright Zona Gale and her friend, William Maxwell. Marjorie Latimer wrote three novels here.

Today, some writers still are hearing about the retreat and come from across the country. But most guests are honeymooners, city families and couples on getaways, plus weddings (Wisconsin wildlife artist Owen Gromme was married in the garden) and business meetings. Guests swim, innertube, picnic by or simply look at the Neenah River, which winds slowly through sandhill crane nesting areas and picnic grounds, near Indian effigy mounds. Bill Schultz bought the estate in 1982 for his late wife, Polly, but understates that he's "taken to it very nicely."

Income from the guest houses is turned back into authentic restoration. The buildings have a bright, clean look. They are comfortably but not luxuriously furnished with antiques from the 1860-90s which Bill and Polly collected and refinished; Polly made the rag rugs. Guests have use of the entire grounds.

Meals: Fix-your-own; the Log House and the Carpenter's Cottage have fully furnished kitchens.

Rooms and Rates: Three guest houses. The 1862 Log House has a living room, dining room, kitchen and bathroom with tub and shower. Upstairs is one sleeping room with six beds (five twins, one double). The Carpenter's Cottage was the carpenter's shop. Living room, kitchen; bedroom has two double beds, bathroom with tub only. Sleeps 4. Tower House has bedroom, fireplaces on first and third floor, third floor is meditation room for all guests, has separate stair; bath in adjacent building with shower only; no kitchen. Rates are $50 single or double. Each additional person, $6. Add tax.

Dates open: April 1 - Nov. 1   **Smoking:** Outside

Children: "If they have respect for furnishings"   **Pets:** No

Nearby: Hiking, snowshoeing, tubing, swimming (rope swing), fishing, picnicking, x-c skiing, campfires, birdwatching, games on the property. Bike maps provided for area roads. Lake Mason fishing, 2 miles. Wisconsin Dells, 11 miles.

Location/Directions: I-90/94 to either Exit 78 (Portage) or Exit 87 (Wisconsin Dells). Follow Highways 51 or 23 respectively to County Road X; turn east on Third Avenue; estate is off Third. Detailed map sent. Chicago, 3 hours. Madison, 1 hour. Milwaukee, 2 hours. Twin Cities, 4.5 hours.

Deposit: First night's lodging

Payment: Cash, personal or traveler's checks only

Baraboo

The Barrister's House
226 Ninth Ave.
P.O. Box 166
Baraboo, WI 53913
608-356-3344

Owners/Operators:
Mary and Glen Schulz
Deanna Schulz, daughter

This brick and wood bluff-top home was built in 1933 by a prominent local attorney, H. Langer. His wife lived here until the early 1970s. At that time, the Langer children were settled in their homes and decided to sell the family home.

An accountant bought the house immediately when it went up for sale. "He had lived across the street and always wanted it," said Deanna Schulz, so he bought it and went home and told his family they were moving back to the old neighborhood. The family room was added to enlarge the space.

In 1984, Mary and Glen Schulz became third owners. They bought the house specifically to run as a B&B. "For their 25th wedding anniversary, they went to the White Lace Inn in Sturgeon Bay and they just loved it," Deanna said. "They thought a B&B would be the perfect early retirement."

But retirement hasn't happened yet, not until she and her brother get out of college, anyway, she said. Mary, a first-grade teacher, and Glen, a school administrator, work in Lodi and run the B&B every weekend. Mary runs it all summer.

When they acquired the home, it was in very good shape. Original wallpaper and wood paneling remains in the library, and the off-white carpet in the living room has remained in great condition since its 1933 installation. They redecorated the dining room, painted the living room and added the private bathrooms.

Since opening in 1984, some of the Langer descendents have come to visit and provide information on the house. Mary, who grew up in Baraboo, remembers coming to the Barrister's House as a girl for a birthday party for one of the daughters.

Rooms and Rates: Four - All upstairs with private baths. The Maid's Room is furnished in 1930s pieces, private bath down the hall with tub and shower - $45. The Garden Room is green and white, overlooks garden, has white iron bed, shower only - $50. The Colonial Room is in golds with 18th century furnishings, shower only - $50. The Barrister's Room has a half-canopy bed, chaise lounge, natural cherry wood and cranberry glass, tub and shower - $55. Sleeping porch can be rented with any of rooms for children who use the bath in their parent's room - $15-25. Singles $5 less. Add tax.

Meals: Continental breakfast served in the dining room in front of black marble fireplace, or on porch or terrace in summer, 8:30-10. It includes homemade sweet rolls and muffins or coffeecake, cheese and crackers and a fruit cup with topping.

Dates open: Daily June through August; weekends only September through May

Smoking: No   **Children:** Yes   **Pets:** No

Nearby: Circus World Museum, 1 mile. Downtown Baraboo, 5 blocks. Devil's Lake State Park (camping, hiking, beaches and boat rentals), 2 miles. International Crane Foundation center (trails, exhibits, tours), 5 miles. Mid-Continent Railway Museum (steam engine train rides), 8 miles. Wisconsin Dells, 12 miles.

Location/Directions: From Highway 33 in Baraboo, turn north one block on Birch Street (one block from Kentucky Fried Chicken) to Ninth. Chicago, 3.5 hours. Madison, 1 hour. Milwaukee, 2 hours. Twin Cities, 4 hours.

Deposit: $25

Payment: Cash, personal or traveler's checks only

Baraboo

House of Seven Gables

215 Sixth St.
P.O. Box 204
Baraboo, WI 53913
608-356-8387

Owners/Operators:
Pam and Ralph Krainik

Ralph Krainik knows the gingerbread and gables on this Carpenter Gothic home so well he could draw them in his sleep. That's because it took five summers to paint all the trim, plus reinforce porches and do other improvments to this tri-color home, listed on the National Register of Historic Places.

The circa-1860 home was built for Baraboo bank president Terrill Thomas, whose family owned it until 1910. Then a Catholic priest, artist and poet bought it as his retirement home. From 1920-62, county judge and district attorney Henry Bohn owned it. In 1932, an artist who happened to be the local minister's wife painted a mural on the den walls, with farm and meadow scenes and an elf in a corner that a Bohn toddler could enjoy.

But before 1966, when the Krainiks purchased it, the home had been used as apartments and was run down, with plywood covering pine floors and red and white-striped aluminum awnings over the windows. "Ralph had just started at a law firm here and we saw it was for sale and jumped at the chance," said Pam. They knew it needed work, but soon found out "the ad was a total lie," and that no major work had been done. "We have spent 21 years doing it and, except for the kitchen, we did everything ourselves."

Today, the house has peach with burgundy and salmon trim exterior and a Victorian garden. The 100 years of old appliances and mattresses stored in the basement are gone, and the nooks and crannies and cupboards and other interesting spaces have been uncovered. The house is furnished in furniture from the 1860-80 period, some of which took years of searching. Ralph built the gazebo.

The House of Seven Gables became a B&B in 1983, when B&Bs were still virtually unheard of in the Midwest. The second bedroom was opened in 1985.

Guests get a tour of the home, complete with stories from Pam or Ralph. They may use the gazebo, the Sunday parlor and living room and dining room.

Rooms and Rates: Two - Both upstairs with private baths and window air conditioning. Victorian Room has a walnut, high-backed bed, done in yellows. Servant's Quarters has maple double bed and three-quarter pine bed, sloping roofs from one of the gables. Baths have clawfoot tubs, no showers. $45 single, $55 double, $5 per child and $10 each additional adult. Add tax.

Meals: Full breakfast is served in dining room (with huge, high-backed Gothic chairs) before 9 or at time arranged night before. It includes an entree of quiche or apple fritters with popovers or homebaked muffins and fresh fruit; tea or coffee can be enjoyed in the gazebo.

Dates open: Year 'round   **Smoking:** No

Children: Yes   **Pets:** No

Nearby: Circus World Museum, 10 blocks. Downtown Baraboo, 2 blocks. Devil's Lake State Park (camping, hiking, beaches and boat rentals), 3 miles. International Crane Foundation center (trails, exhibits, tours), 5 miles. Mid-Continent Railway Museum (steam engine train rides), 8 miles. Wisconsin Dells, 10 miles.

Location/Directions: From Highway 33 in Baraboo, turn south on East Street two blocks to Sixth. Chicago, 3.5 hours. Madison, 1 hour. Milwaukee, 2 hours. Twin Cities, 4 hours.

Deposit: Half of room rate or confirmation by credit card

Payment: Cash, traveler's checks, VISA or MasterCard

Wisconsin Dells

B&B House on River Road
922 River Road
Wisconsin Dells, WI 53965
608-253-5573

Owners/Operators:
Jane and Marlin Waldrop

The land on which this 100-year-old home was built at one time was owned by Kilbourn, the city founder and man after whom the town was named until the 1930s. Its location, a block from downtown and on the street next to the Wisconsin River, suggests Kilbourn knew its value as a building site.

In 1890, Adolf Rothe, a Kilbourn banker, purchased the site and built the house for his family. He had three children and the home was built large, with plenty of bedrooms.

Over the years it served other families, too, and in 1970 it was purchased as a family home by Jane Waldrop. When she married Marlin Waldrop in 1983, they suddenly had a farm, this large house and, most recently, an apartment above a gift shop downtown in which to live.

In the summer of 1985, they opened the B&B after reading about them and their increasing popularity. Seven guest rooms are available, but only four are rented at any one time. The Waldrops live in the house when guests are present.

Over the years, a number of improvements have been necessary. Wood floors have been refinished. The house has been rewired and replumbed, and new bathrooms added. Electric heat has replaced the radiators.

Natural woodwork remains, and the Waldrops continue to uncover more of the home's original decor (the cabinets in the kitchen, for example, were just stripped). The furnishings are antiques and collectibles the couple has gathered; they also sell antiques at a local antique mall.

Guests have use of the dining room, living room and front porch and lawn, from which some of the river can be seen.

Rooms and Rates: Seven - Four rented at once, all have window air conditioners. Downstairs, the Pine Room and Parlor Room have sliding doors to make a suite; they share a bath (or have a private bath if rented alone) with shower only - $55 each. Upstairs: Maple Room has twin maple beds - $50. Walnut Room is done in blues, has double walnut bed - $40. Rose Room has a family heirloom brass bed - $45. Oak Room has an oak chair and brass bed - $35. Birch Room is done in beige and has two double antique beds - $40 for two, $50 with children. Bath down the hall has clawfoot tub with shower. Each additional person on rollway cot, $10. Add tax.

Meals: Continental breakfast is served in the kitchen, dining room or on the front porch 8-9 and includes fruit cup, croissants, Danish or English muffin.

Dates open: May 1 - Nov. 1   **Smoking:** Prefer not in guestrooms

Children: Yes   **Pets:** No

Nearby: Upper Dells boat rides, 1 block. Lower Dells boat rides, 4 blocks. Downtown (restaurants, fudge shops, amusements), 2 blocks.

Location/Directions: Exit 87 from I-90/94; go over river and into downtown to first stop light, turn left. Turn left at next corner to alley, turn right to house next to motel units. Chicago, 3.5 hours. Madison, 1 hour. Milwaukee, 2 hours. Twin Cities, 4 hours.

Deposit: First night's lodging

Payment: Cash, personal or traveler's checks, VISA or MasterCard

Wisconsin Dells

Historic Bennett House
825 Oak St.
Wisconsin Dells, WI 53965
608-254-2500

Owner/Operator:
Patricia Zolla

Back in 1863, when Jacob Weber built this home, Wisconsin Dells was called Kilbourn and the undammed Wisconsin River flowed freely close by.

With the lumbermen flocking to the area came H.H. Bennett, who bought the house in 1891. Bennett was to become a famous nature photographer who first recorded the natural beauty of the rock formations along the river. He did developing and printing of his photos in the house until he opened his studio down the street, a shop now run by his granddaughter. Today, some of his works are in the Smithsonian Institution and the house is on the National Register of Historic Places. The Bennett family owned the house until 1971.

As the Dells grew, the house, located just one block from downtown, faced the wrecking ball. Charles Thompson, a local restaurant owner, stepped in to save it and the house next door. "This man poured a fortune into the house," said Pat Zolla, who bought it from him in 1984. He rewired, replumbed, fixed crumbling walls and redecorated in period pieces, finally opening the home for tours.

That's how Pat Zolla first saw the home. "About 18 years ago, I went to Europe and traveled B&Bs with a friend. I worked for Sears as a decorator then, and I started looking for B&Bs when I traveled." Then she found herself looking for old homes with the idea of opening a B&B herself. When she toured the Thompson house, she knew that was the right place. She bought it and considers herself lucky Thompson did so much work on it. Her B&B opened in early 1985.

Guests have use of the living and dining rooms and the back porch, screened in for summer. TVs are available in four of five rooms.

Rooms and Rates: Five - Four rented at once. Downstairs, a suite has double brass bed, sitting room with sofa sleeper and private bath with shower only - $60 double, $45 after Labor Day. Upstairs, all with hardwood floors: Pink room has two twin beds arranged foot-to-foot, green spreads. Green Room has double antique bed. Blue Room has lace curtains, double bed. Red room has white wicker headboard and double bed. All share bath with clawfoot tub only. $45 doubles, $35 singles; $10 less after Labor Day. Each additional person, $5. Add tax.

Meals: Breakfast is served in the dining room 8-9:30 and might include western omelettes, bacon, hash browns, toast and strawberries, or pancakes, scrambled eggs, sausage and coffee cake. "The coffee pot is always on and cookie jar is always full," to which guests can help themselves in the hall.

Dates open: Year 'round

Smoking: Not in guest rooms

Children: Over 12

Pets: No

Nearby: Upper Dells boat rides, 1 block. Lower Dells boat rides, 3 blocks. Downtown (restaurants, fudge shops and amusements), 1 block.

Location/Directions: Take Exit 87 from I-90/94; go over river and into downtown to first stop light, turn left one block. House is on corner. Parking in the rear. Chicago, 3.5 hours. Madison, 1 hour. Milwaukee, 2 hours. Twin Cities, 4 hours.

Deposit: Half of first night's lodging

Payment: Cash, personal or traveler's checks, VISA or MasterCard

Wisconsin Dells

Sherman House

930 River Road
P.O. Box 397
Wisconsin Dells, WI 53965
608-253-2721

Owner/Operator:
Norma Marz

As a child, Norma Marz can remember her sister riding a bicycle up to the neighbor's huge native sandstone porch, right across it, and down the other side.

Today, that porch is screened in and Marz owns it. At the time, however, it was owned by J.M. Sherman, a Chicago attorney who had the 14-room house overlooking the Upper Wisconsin River built as a summer home. Little Norma, born on the same street "a little further down," and her sister used to play with the children who were guests of the Crandalls, the second owners. They bought the place in the 1930s, about the time the town changed its name from Kilbourn.

The Crandall family owned a hotel in town and for a short period used this eight-bedroom place as an annex. Crandalls also owned a lot of riverfront land along the Upper Dells as well as the Dells Boat Company, which, along with the house, were left to the Wisconsin Alumni Research Foundation of the University of Wisconsin.

In 1974, Marz and her husband came back to the Dells and bought the home from the Foundation, for whom upkeep had been too much. At the time, the Marzs had five children in school and needed the space. Her husband died in 1982 and the children have left home. "You know," she says, "I think I started the B&B to justify keeping this place."

The home is done in the clean, classic lines of Prairie School architecture, and it was featured in a 1905 "House Beautiful" magazine. Robert Spencer, the architect, was an associate of Frank Lloyd Wright.

From the porch or living room, guests can see the river leading to the Upper Dells. A park bench in the small park next to the house also provides a good view.

The living room, porch, dining room, kitchen and music room are open to guests. About 5 p.m., pop, lemonade and coffee are served to guests for a tea-time that's "pretty relaxed."

Rooms and Rates: Four - All upstairs. The family suite is done in dark greens and has a double bed plus two twin beds; private bath has a shower and separate tub - $60. Peach room has a double bed; bath with tub and shower is shared with Green Room. Green Room has a river view and triple bay windows. $35 single, $45 double. Add tax.

Meals: Continental breakfast is served on the porch in the dining room or in the kitchen at a time arranged the night before. It may include rolls and cereal; guests staying several days are served a full breakfast.

Dates open: May 1 - Nov. 1   **Smoking:** Yes (owner does)

Children: Yes   **Pets:** No

Nearby: Upper Dells boat trips, 1 block. Lower Dells boat trips, 4 blocks. Downtown (restaurants, fudge shops and amusements), 2 blocks.

Location/Directions: Exit 87 from I-90/94; go over river and into downtown to first stop light, turn left. Turn left at next corner to alley, turn right to end of alley. No parking on River Road; park behind house. Chicago, 3.5 hours. Madison, 1 hour. Milwaukee, 2 hours. Twin Cities, 4 hours.

Deposit: None

Payment: Cash, personal or traveler's checks only

000# Stevens Point

The Victorian Swan on Water
1716 Water St.
Stevens Point, WI 54481
715-345-0595

Owners: Joan Ouellette,
Chuck and Mary Egle
Operator: Joan Ouellette

This huge house took many years getting where it is today, but Joan Ouellette took only one day to decide it was the place for her B&B.

Started in 1888, the home took three years to build. It was designed by Boston architect Frank B. Smith for Philip Rothman, the owner of local dry goods stores. And it was built in another part of town on Clark Street.

It was then owned by the Olsen family, owners and operators of a fuel company. Henry Olsen bought it in 1938 when the building needed to be moved from the land owned by Sentry Insurance.

To move it, "they took off the third story and cut the house in half," says Ouellette, who wishes she could have been around to see it. "I've been told they had to lift electrical wires all along the way."

Then the home was turned into a duplex and rented out. Finally, George Guyant bought it and began restoration, but he was transferred and had to sell.

"I've been in service jobs most of my life and I like people and I like to cook," says Ouellette, who was then living in Milwaukee. "I told my brother (Chuck Egle) living here that I wanted to open a B&B." He soon called her back, asking if she was serious, and said he would help her find a house in Stevens Point, having this one in mind. "It took one day to find the house," she said, "but zoning took six months." After buying it in June 1986, she and Egle worked on the rest of the restoration. "The black walnut parquet floors were covered with a lot of gook," she explained. Interesting original fixtures remain.

She has photos that show guests some of the stripping and other work required, and she points out the spot where the house was cut in half for the move. The black cherry fireplace in the living room works and is available for guests, as is the TV room. The large parlors can be closed off and used as small business meeting rooms or for receptions.

Rooms and Rates: Four - All private baths. Newport-Chaney Room is done in peach, has queen bed, turret windows, shower only - $53. The Balcony Room has grey iron double bed with lilac comforter, antique lace curtains, bath has shower only - $43. Crystal Dawn Room has twin beds, clawfoot tub and shower - $43. Rothman Room has double bed, bath downstairs with walnut and birdseye maple wainscotting, clawfoot tub and shower - $38. Singles $3 less. Add tax.

Meals: Breakfast is served family-sytle in the sun room 7-9 or by agreement reached the night before. It may include French toast stuffed with cream cheese, meat, fresh fruit and muffins or quiche, scrambled eggs or pancakes and sticky buns.

Dates open: Year 'round   **Smoking:** No

Children: Over 12   **Pets:** No

Nearby: Downtown, 4 blocks. Wisconsin River (x-c skiing, picnic areas, ice skating and walking trails), 4 blocks. Sentry golf course, 1.5 miles, and five others within 25 minutes. Farmer's Market (open all week in summer), 5 blocks.

Location/Directions: Look for the Stevens Point water tower -- B&B is directly below it. Chicago, 4.5 hours. Madison, 1.5 hours. Milwaukee, 3 hours. Twin Cities, 4 hours.

Deposit: First night's lodging

Payment: Cash, personal or traveler's checks, VISA or MasterCard

Wausau

Rosenberry Inn

511 Franklin
Wausau, WI 54401
715-842-5733

Owners/Operators:
Patty and Jerry Artz
Doug Artz, son

When Patty and Jerry Artz looked for an historic home in Wausau to remodel into a B&B, they had their sights set on a white Victorian mansion on Franklin Street. But when they discovered it had few rooms and plenty of work, they looked at a property just down the street they didn't think they'd consider. The green stucco home was "prairie school" architecture - clean lines, nothing full of gingerbread or other decoration. "It was modernized paneling and drop ceilings," cut into eight tiny studio apartments back in the '40s and not very attractive.

But the eight rooms already had bathrooms and kitchenettes, a plus for a B&B. They liked the woodwork that remained. When they bought the home in January 1985, it was part of the 61-property Andrew Warren Historic District and listed on the National Register of Historic Places. The Artz's were determined to restore it to a condition of which its original owner would have been proud.

That owner was Marvin Rosenberry, a chief justice of the Wisconsin Supreme Court for 21 years, and Kate, his wife. The house was built in 1908, during Wausau's lumber boom, when neighbors were lumber barons and merchants.

The Artz's turned the third floor into their apartment and guest lounge, where guests eat breakfast. The Wisconsin antiques they've collected for years decorate the guest rooms. Restoration included removing four to five coats of wallpaper and paint, indoor-outdoor carpeting, drop ceilings, modern paneling and replacing showers and tubs. Original stained glass windows and doors remain.

A huge porch with swing also is available for guests.

Rooms and Rates: Eight - All with private bath (some with shower only), kitchenettes, hardwood floors with rag rugs. Working fireplaces in rooms 1, 2, 5 and 6. Examples include: Room 1 was the library, has a built-in bookcase, white iron double bed. Room 4 has a double bed, plus two twin beds on a sunporch, and a window seat. Room 7 is two twins with mallards on the wallpaper. Room 8 has antique bed, clawfoot tub and shower. $40 single, $45 double. Each additional person, $10. Add tax.

Meals: Continental breakfast is served in the gathering room or guest room and it includes rolls and banana bread and sometimes fruit.

Dates open: Year 'round   **Smoking:** Yes

Children: Yes   **Pets:** No

Nearby: Parks, Wisconsin River, theater, shopping mall, antique shops, gift shops, restaurants, 4-6 blocks to downtown; Dells of Eau Claire falls and park, 15 miles; ski hill and x-c ski trails, 4-5 miles. Leigh Yawkey Woodson Art Museum, Historical Society, 2-3 blocks.

Location/Directions: Located in town near Sixth and Franklin (follow Highway 52 east). Chicago, 5 hours. Madison, 2.5 hours. Milwaukee, 3 hours. Twin Cities, 3.5 hours.

Deposit: Not necessary

Payment: Cash, personal or traveler's checks, VISA or MasterCard

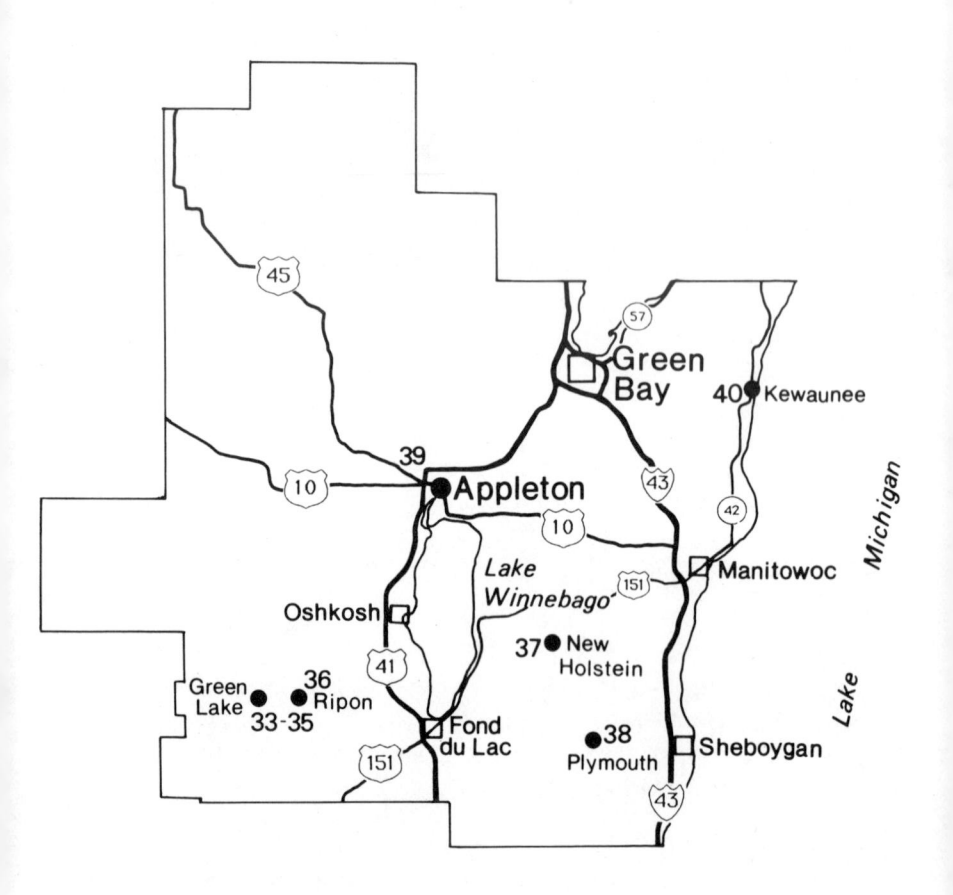

-East Wisconsin Waters

33. McConnell Inn - Green Lake.. 96-97
34. Oakwood Lodge - Green Lake.. 98-99
35. Strawberry Hill B&B - Green Lake................................100-101
36. The Farmer's Daughter Inn - Ripon............................. 102-103
37. The Farm Homestead - New Holstein......................... 104-105
38. 52 Stafford, An Irish Guest House - Plymouth.............. 106-107
39. The Parkside - Appleton...108-109
40. The Gables - Kewaunee...110-111

Green Lake

McConnell Inn

497 S. Lawson Dr. (Business 23)
Green Lake, WI 54941
414-294-6430

Owners/Operators:
Mary Jo and Scott Johnson

Mary Jo and Scott Johnson had lived out East and in Chicago, but they wanted to come back to their Wisconsin roots. Buying a 1901 Victorian probably was not the easiest way, but the renovation necessary didn't change their minds.

It took two years to build this house for John and Josephine McConnell, inlaying the parquet floors piece by piece and handtooling the leather wainscotting found in the dining room. It didn't take quite that long to get the B&B ready to open, but the six months of work were very busy. After years of changing hands and finally ending up owned by college students, major work was needed.

"The plumbing lines in the basement were every which way," Mary Jo said, and then there was the basement cistern to deal with. "Gutters were still pouring water in the cistern and it was full -- we had to pump it out and reroute the gutter." The cistern held water for the house's unusual gravity-powered water supply. Moving in before Scott could, Mary Jo ripped up the carpet, its pad and a layer of linoleum and renewed the parquet floors. New insulation was put in, the house was rewired and the woodwork around the windows was stripped.

Today, Mary Jo says she still isn't finished. Now she wants to concentrate on the exterior. But inside, the house looks "done" to guests. It's decorated with family heirlooms, like a trunk her ancestors carried across the Atlantic.

Mary Jo, a pastry chef, and Scott, a real estate appraiser, both have talents that come in handy. (Plus, they've traveled a lot of B&Bs out East and love the experience.) Homebaked English muffins (a far cry from the store-bought kind) and other treats are on the breakfast menu. Also, Mary Jo teaches breadbaking from the house. She offers short weekend courses when the weather is cool.

Guests can watch TV downstairs, read or play games. A cooler is available to fishermen. Candies are in all rooms and fresh flowers are, too, in the summer.

Rooms and Rates: Four - All have lake view, one double bed, and are decorated in family heirloom antiques. Turret bedroom has whitewashed floors, private bath with clawfoot tub and shower - $50. Master bedroom is done in blues and has private bath with clawfoot tub and shower - $50. Green room has braided rug, old kitchen utensils on the wall - $40. Stencil room has hand-stenciled floor, done in rose colors - $40. Green and stencil room share a bath with clawfoot tub and shower. Add tax. Weekly rates.

Meals: Breakfast is served in the dining room or to the guest rooms 8:30-9:30 or at an earlier time arranged the night before. It includes a homemade pastry, baked fresh that morning, fresh fruit, cold cereals and homemade English muffins in summer. In cooler months, expect apple cheese pancakes, or zucchini nut bread French toast, oatmeal or hot cereal. Jams, jellies and some juices are homemade.

Dates open: Year 'round   **Smoking:** On porch only

Children: Over 15   **Pets:** No

Nearby: Marina with boat rental, boat launch across street. Shops, restaurants, churches, 2 blocks. Three parks with bandshell, picnic grounds, fishing, playgrounds, Green Lake city beach, 3 blocks. Three golf courses within 5 miles. Green Lake Conference Center (x-c skiing), 2 miles.

Location/Directions: Large Victorian house located on northwest side of Highway 23 (business route) by the lake. Chicago, 3 hours. Madison, 1.5 hours. Milwaukee, 1.5 hours. Twin Cities, 5.5 hours.

Deposit: Full amount for one night stays; half of room rate or confirmation by credit card for extended stays

Payment: Cash, personal or traveler's checks, VISA or MasterCard

Green Lake

Oakwood Lodge
365 Lake St.
Green Lake, WI 54941
414-294-6580

Owner/Operator:
Marcy Klepinger

In 1866, when David Greenway bought 2,000 feet of lake frontage and 35 acres here, building a resort this far west was no small endeavor. His workmen got to the site each day on a trail blazed the eight miles from Ripon. Duties were rotated so one man was responsible each day for shooting game and making dinner.

The Oakwood Hotel that Greenway was building was the first summer resort on Green Lake and said to be the first west of Niagara. Greenway came to Wisconsin in 1850 at the age of 24, settling in Ripon as a farmer, then he operated a drug store and was an agent for Livingston and Fargo Express Co. for 15 years.

When the first resort building opened with accommodations for 75 guests, it was a bigger hit than even Greenway expected. Other buildings and cottages were commissioned to serve guests now coming from New Orleans, St. Louis and Memphis. The main lodge was three stories with a huge veranda and gazebo. The first floor held dining rooms and the kitchen. The second had parlors, an office and a barbershop. The third had guest rooms and a telegraph system with an operator. The grounds boasted a greenhouse, gardens, laundry and stables for the horses which were picking up guests at the railroad in Ripon.

Greenway sold the resort in 1890 and retired. Ten years later, times were not so good for the pioneer resort. The wooden buildings were badly in need of difficult and expensive modernization. By 1929, it had changed hands several times since the turn of the century, and the glorious old hotel was razed. About that time, the land was divided into lots. Some of the guest cottages were moved to Lake Street.

The largest guest cottage is Oakwood Lodge today. Marcy Klepinger has owned it for three years, decorated it with her own antiques and kept the resort business alive. A small restaurant is on the first floor, as is a large screened-in porch and TV room. Guests can also use a family room on the lower level and the private pier and raft in the lake.

Rooms and Rates: 10 - Examples include: #1, downstairs, pine floor, king brass bed, private bath with tub and shower, decorated in antiques - $44; #9, upstairs, one double and one twin bed, bay window overlooking lake, sink in room, shares bath - $42. $39-47 doubles; singles $5 less. Each additional person, $5; cribs, $3. Two-night minimum required May 1-Oct. 30; three-night minimum holiday weekends. Add tax. Weekly and group rate.

Meals: Breakfast included in room rates Nov. 1-April 30. Breakfast is served in the dining room and may include buttermilk pancakes, omelettes, coffee cake or sweet rolls. The dining room is open to the public for breakfast 7-11 weekdays, May through October, and 7-12 weekends, year 'round.

Dates open: Closed two weeks in both November and March

Smoking: Yes   **Children:** Yes   **Pets:** No

Nearby: Private pier and raft for swimming, boating, sunning. Shops, restaurants, churches, down the street. Three golf courses within 10 miles. Green Lake Conference Center (x-c skiing), 2 miles.

Location/Directions: Follow Lake Street along shore from town. Detailed map sent. Chicago, 3 hours. Madison, 1.5 hours. Milwaukee, 1.5 hours. Twin Cities, 5.5 hours.

Deposit: First night's lodging

Payment: Cash, personal or traveler's checks only

Green Lake

Strawberry Hill B&B

Rt. 1, Box 524-D
Green Lake, WI 54941
414-294-3450

Owner/Operator:
Patricia Spencer

Pat Spencer had been thinking about opening a B&B for years, but little did she think she'd end up doing that in Green Lake, Wisconsin.

Though from the area originally, Spencer had been living in California. In 1985, she came back to Green Lake to work as a full-time volunteer for one year for the Heifer Project, a 40-year-old interfaith agency that provides farm animals to farmers in developing countries. "I traveled 1,500 miles a month that year," she recalls, explaining the program to Wisconsin farmers and recruiting support. "I really didn't know what I'd do at the end of that year." Finding the house for sale was the best excuse to stay. "I saw this house and I had to have it."

The farmhouse is perched on a knoll a good block back from the highway. For years, the farm belonged to the Zobel family, and two daughters lived in the farmhouse. Spencer is the fourth or fifth owner, buying it from a doctor and his wife, who kept sheep, turkeys, guinea hens and geese.

"Everyone's taken pretty good care of the place. I redecorated and that was it." Previous owners had added air conditioning and a glassed-in sun porch, complete with hot tub, which guests may use. The porch has a view of the strawberry patch, the barn and surrounding fields. The strawberry patch has been carried inside, in a way, with strawberry wallpaper in the dining room. "Much of the produce is raised on the place and guests are welcome to purchase surplus garden truck." The farm animals are no longer present, and the only animal is a Doberman that added security in California but has mellowed into nearly a lap-dog on the stress-free farm. Hardwood floors have been preserved throughout, including the pine and red fir floors upstairs.

Spencer opened the B&B in 1986. "Guests have the run of the house," including use of the living room, and play horseshoes and croquet on the lawn, or lounge in the hammock. Fresh flowers are placed in rooms during the summer.

Rooms and Rates: Four - All upstairs, sharing two baths, one with tub and shower, other with shower only. Red room has double bed, done in red calico print wallpaper. Butterfly room has butterflies on the walls, double bed, faces southwest. King room has pink walls, grey carpet and comforter. Canine room has dog wallpaper borders, two twin white iron beds, sloping roof, sitting area with binoculars. $20 single, $35 double. Add tax.

Meals: Breakfast is served in the dining room or on the solar porch at a time arranged night before. It starts with a strawberry dacquiri (from her own strawberries, of course) and includes Baurenfruhstruck (German farmer's breakfast of stir-fied potatoes, green pepper, onion and cheese), sausage and sourdough biscuits, or waffles or strata.

Dates open: Year 'round

Smoking: No

Children: Over 11

Pets: No

Nearby: Downtown Green Lake shops, restaurants, beach, boat rentals, 2 miles. Canoeing, half-mile. Three golf courses within 6 miles. Fur and leather shops in Berlin, fishing and boating Fox River, 8 miles. Mecan River canoe rentals, 20 miles. Good biking from farm.

Location/Directions: From Highway 23, turn north for a half-mile, house is on the right. Chicago, 3 hours. Madison, 1.5 hours. Milwaukee, 1.5 hours. Twin Cities, 5.5 hours.

Deposit: Half of room rate

Payment: Cash, personal or traveler's checks only

Ripon

The Farmer's Daughter Inn

Route 1, Box 37
Ripon, WI 54971
414-748-2146

Owners/Operators:
Donna and Dwain Werch

No TV. No radio. No telephone. Board games. Lawn games. Picnics. Sound like heaven? Donna Werch's guests think so. At her Farmer's Daughter Inn, a five-bedroom farmhouse which guests rent out, the privacy and quiet are big drawing cards for harried families who can't remember the last time they spent an evening together without someone turning on the TV.

In 1847, when this land was homesteaded, no one would have guessed that visitors would want to come to watch milking, ring a huge dinner bell or just watch the corn and peas grow. But city folks, especially, want to do just that.

Donna's father-in-law bought the 320-acre farm in the 1940s. Over the years, the family lived in either this farmhouse or the one down the road, where they live today, renting this one out. Then, Donna said, an annual event in Oshkosh led to opening a one-week-per-year B&B. "I had been taking people in for bed-and-breakfast during the Experimental Aircraft Association convention in 1983 and 1984. We had a good time with them -- I just enjoy people." The decision was soon made to open a slightly different version year 'round in the second farmhouse.

New wiring and other improvements were made after the last renters moved out, and the guest house opened in 1985. Guests bring their own volleyball net and other lawn games. They come down to Donna's place where her sons help a youngster (or adult, for that matter) bottle feed a calf. Her farm has dogs and cats and chickens, and guests can see milking equipment and walk in the fields.

The house is rented to only one family or party at one time. The houses are separated by fields of sweet corn and peas so guests have privacy. A playroom, crib, high chair, jumping horse and games are provided. If guests wish, Donna will supply food ordered in advance so the cupboards are stocked when they arrive; guests then reimburse her. Two TV interviews featuring the inn can be sent on videotape to prospective guests. Special tours of area farms also can be arranged.

Rooms and Rates: Five bedrooms - Entire house rented. Upstairs has four bedrooms, one with double bed and one twin, one with double bed and crib, one with one twin, and one with double bed; one twin bed downstairs. Bathroom has tub and shower. $65 per night for six. Each additional person, $10. Add tax. Weekly rates.

Meals: Cook-your-own in farmhouse kitchen. Full kitchen is stocked with popcorn, coffee and canned milk, plus linens and utensils. Donna will go shopping before guests arrive if a grocery list is provided and she is reimbursed.

Dates open: Year 'round   **Smoking:** Yes

Children: Yes   **Pets:** No

Nearby: Rippin' Good Cookies factory tours and outlet store, 1.5 miles. Ripon College, 2 miles. Gothic millpond and park, 3 miles. Green Lake (fishing, boating, swimming), 7 miles. Three golf courses within 12 miles. Oshkosh and Lake Winnebago, 20 miles. Horicon Marsh wildlife refuge, 30 miles.

Location/Directions: From Highway 23 southeast of town, take Douglas Street north of Ripon to Locust Road. Turn right; house is second place on the left. Chicago, 3 hours. Madison, 1.5 hours. Milwaukee, 1.5 hours. Twin Cities, 6 hours.

Deposit: $25 per night

Payment: Cash, personal or traveler's checks only

New Holstein

The Farm Homestead
W1982 Kiel Road, Route 2
New Holstein, WI 53061
414-782-5421 reservations
414-894-3195 farm

Owners/Operators:
Family of Caroline and
Joe Krupp

The three sisters and three brothers who have opened this farmhouse B&B are the fourth generation on the family farm. Sections of farm date back to 1858, about the time Marion Marsh's great-grandparents came here from Germany. This area is known as "the Holy Land" -- nearby towns are St. Ann's, Jericho and Marytown, for instance. There were similar farm areas in Germany, Marsh said.

"All of us grew up on this farm. My father lived here with his parents and they had 12 kids," she said. "This was always a source of retreat for those of us who live in the city." Sitting in the living room in front of a crackling fire, it's no wonder. The room has a beamed ceiling with hand-hewn logs from the old barn and is full of family heirlooms and dried flowers. The dining room has its original tin ceiling, and the house is decorated with furniture her mother refinished.

What to do with the house became a family decision after both parents had died. A brother still farms and has milking cows, but he lives in his own house and something had to be done with the family farmhouse. "I thought of a home for older adults," said Marsh, a nurse. They got as far as interviewing families to live on site with the adults when it was time for the annual fall trip by the three sisters. They went to The Inn in Montreal and asked Schumacher's advice on opening a B&B. Schumachers gave encouragement. The B&B opened in March 1987, with one of the sisters or brothers on hand when guests are there.

"We tell them the whole house is theirs. They can make their own coffee and use the fridge." A picnic table is available out in back, and guests can also visit the dairy barn.

Rooms and Rates: Five - Four rented out at once. All upstairs with antiques and some modern decor in paneling, floor or ceilings. Green room has double bed, crib with handmade quilt, Mom's cedar chest with daughters' old wool skirts, dresser Grandma carved. Large room has two double beds, sloping roof, two windows and Grandma's table. Yellow room has Mom's sewing machine, double bed with Mom's knotted yellow quilt. Small beige room has antique carved double bed and old Zenith radio. Fifth room has double bed, pull-chain light. All share half-bath upstairs. Second bath has tub and shower (shower in basement, also). $25 single, $40 double. Add tax.

Meals: Breakfast is served at a time arranged the night before in the dining room, or on the screened porch or picnic table. It's the "breakfast mom always made for the family:" bacon pieces in scrambled eggs, homemade muffins, whole wheat raisin or honey oat toast with homemade bread. Special diets can be accommodated.

Dates open: Year 'round

Smoking: Not in guest rooms

Children: Yes

Pets: "Prefer not"

Nearby: Restaurants, craft shops, 2 miles. Fishing, golf, snowmobiling, hiking, x-c skiing within 10 miles; downhill skiing, 15 miles. Ledge View Nature Center, 10 miles. Historic Wade House (Wisconsin Historic Site), 12 miles. Road America track, Elkhart Lake, 10 miles. Northern Kettle Moraine State Forest, 12 miles.

Location/Directions: From Highway 57, take Highway 149 west to Kiel Road, continue straight west when 149 turns right. Third house on right is B&B. Map sent. Chicago, 3 hours. Madison, 2 hours. Milwaukee, 1.5 hours. Twin Cities, 7.5 hours.

Deposit: Half of room rate

Payment: Cash, personal or traveler's checks only

Plymouth

52 Stafford, "An Irish Guest House"

52 Stafford St.
P.O. Box 565
Plymouth, WI 53073
414-893-0552

Owners/Operators:
    Christine and Cary O'Dwanny
Innkeeper:
    Moira Rossow

What makes it all worthwhile for Cary O'Dwanny, whom everyone knows as "Rip," is when a guest, tired from the road or business, "comes through the door, drops the suitcases and just says, 'Wow.' "

There's plenty to "wow" about. O'Dwanny is a young, retired stockbroker who is getting a charge out of putting new life in old buildings around the state (his are also the Inn at Pine Terrace, Oconomowoc, the Audubon Inn in Mayville and the Rochester Inn in Sheboygan Falls). He and his partners have redone this old hotel as an Irish guest house. It's not just Irish because he is, but because settlers were Irish, and their names can be found on tombstones from the 1790s.

Now, Irish names on custom-made stained glass windows in the pub are just one "wow." Standing in the doorway, the pub is to the left, hotel desk to the right, and dark wood staircase ahead. Leaded and etched glass are all over the first floor, including an unusual window in the fireplace near the pub (the flue splits to go around the window). The lobby's carpeting is from England, the silk in the parlor chairs is from China. The cherry woodwork gleams. At the pub, patrons can order a Guinness or all seven Irish whiskeys imported into America; some come regularly to do so, from a block away and from Chicago. Live music is offered some weekends. St. Patrick's Day goes on for 17 days, with music and a parade.

Don't look for green beer, shamrocks or leprechauns. O'Dwanny wanted guests from Ireland and England to truly feel at home here. The $1.4 million restoration involved the use of the original blueprints of the old hotel, continuously operating since 1892 and listed on the National Register of Historic Places. When work began after the purchase in 1985, the boarding house was gutted, reinsulated, rewired, and given new plumbing and heating systems. When the doors opened in April 1986, no detail was forgotten, right down to the Irish Spring soap.

Rooms and Rates: 20 - All have queen four-poster beds with handmade comforters, private baths with tub and shower (17 with whirlpools), cable TV, phones, and are done in various wallpapers and colors. $55 rooms have tubs with showers. $65 rooms have single whirlpools. $75 rooms have double whirlpools. $85 rooms have double whirlpool and are more spacious, such as #9 with four bay windows, couch. Rates are singles or doubles. Additional person, $10. Add tax.

Meals: Continental breakfast is served buffet-style "almost all morning" in the breakfast room and includes muffins, bread pudding, fruit and cold cereal. Sandwiches, soups, pizza, salads, daily specials and desserts are served at the pub.

Dates open: Year 'round   **Smoking:** In some guest rooms

Children: "Well-behaved"   **Pets:** "Well-behaved"

Nearby: Northern Kettle Moraine State Forest (hiking, camping, birdwatching), 5 miles. Road America racing track in Elkhart Lake, 5 miles. Old Wade House (Wisconsin Historic Site), 6 miles. X-c skiing at Greenbush (25+ miles of trails), 6 miles. Kohler Design Center tours, 10 miles. U-pick farms, fishing, snowmobile trails, biking. "We have no fudge shops."

Location/Directions: Take Highways 23 or 67 into downtown Plymouth. Inn is on Stafford near corner of Mill Street. Map sent. Chicago, 2.5 hours. Madison, 2 hours. Milwaukee, 45 minutes. Twin Cities, 6.5 hours.

Deposit: Deposit necessary for race weekends or confirmation by credit card

Payment: Cash, personal or traveler's checks, VISA, MasterCard or AMEX

Appleton

The Parkside
402 E. North St.
Appleton, WI 54911
414-733-0200

Owner/Operator:
Bonnie Riley

Harry Houdini and Edna Ferber once lived in the neighborhood where Dina, Minnie and Anna Geenan were deeded land on which to build a house.

Their father and the three girls owned Appleton's first department store. Originally a dry goods store, they enlarged it to Geenan's Department Store. Their home was located just a few blocks from the downtown store. The three sisters lived in the home until the early 1940s when their new house, just east of the big house, was completed. Soon after, they deeded the original house to a niece. During World War II, an apartment was put in on the third floor for their children as they married.

In 1961, the 1906 home was purchased by new owners. The owners' mother lived independently in the upper apartment for 15 years.

When Bonnie Riley and her family moved to Appleton in 1984, she looked at the home with its potential for a B&B in mind. When she grew up, she spent summers working in the tourism business in Lake Geneva, and "that gave me my first hint I would enjoy something like this." Friends returning from European travels for years had raved about B&Bs, and she believed Appleton could use one. This house, located only a few blocks from Lawrence University and downtown businesses and attractions, had the location and the space.

The third floor apartment which had served the previous two owners became a B&B suite in 1985. It had been unused for at least a decade, Riley estimates, and needed new plumbing, repainting and flooring. In addition to a large living area and kitchenette, the suite has a reading nook overlooking the park. Original leaded glass throughout the house remains. Fresh fruit is waiting in the suite for guests, who also have use of the first floor living and dining rooms. Guests may help themselves to hot coffee downstairs, where the pot is always on. While they may use the kitchenette, breakfast is served by Bonnie downstairs in the dining room, or to the room on a breakfast tray.

Rooms and Rates: One - Located on third floor. Large suite has living room area with oak floor, sofa and dining room table. Bedroom is done in greens, looks out over park and has two twins or one king bed. Private bath with shower only. Kitchen is stocked with coffee, instant soup, wine and soda pop. $50 single, $60 double. Each additional person, $10. Add tax.

Meals: Breakfast is served in the dining room or served upstairs on a tray at a time arranged the night before. It includes fresh fruit, hot popovers or muffins with homemade preserves, cheese and eggs to order.

Dates open: Year 'round

Smoking: No cigars

Children: Over 8

Pets: No

Nearby: City park (picnicking, tennis courts, playground), across street. Downtown, 3 blocks. Lawrence University, 2 blocks. County historical museum, 2 blocks. Lawrence University Conservatory of Music and Drama Center, Chapel, 2 blocks.

Location/Directions: From U.S. 41, take College Ave. (exit 125) about 3 miles through downtown to Drew Street. Turn left, go past city park to North Street. The Parkside is on corner. Chicago, 3.5 hours. Madison, 1.5 hours. Milwaukee, 2 hours. Twin Cities, 6 hours.

Deposit: First night's lodging

Payment: Cash, personal or traveler's checks only

Kewaunee

The Gables
821 Dodge St.
Kewaunee, WI 54216
414-388-0220

Owners/Operators:
Penny and Earl Dunbar

When Earl Dunbar was in Kewaunee on a routine sales call one summer day in 1986, the last thing he had on his mind was looking for another old home that he and Penny might turn into a B&B. They already had looked at between 50 and 100 houses, mostly in Green Bay, and couldn't find one that both they and the city could agree upon to be a B&B. But "here was this big old house sitting on a corner with a for sale sign on it," Earl said, and he couldn't ignore it.

At first glance, the place wasn't much to look at, having sat empty for two years and with a garden and shrubs so overgrown the Dunbars could barely climb the steps. But here was a 22-room Queen Anne Victorian, built in 1883-85 for George and Bertha Grimmer. Grimmer owned a sawmill and was the first state senator for Northeast Wisconsin. His handcrafted home took two years to finish.

Edmund and Sylvia Classon bought the home from the Grimmers and owned it until Sylvia died in 1978. Sylvia was the daughter of Frank Hamachek, the inventor and patenter of the pea harvester, and owner of Hamachek Machinery. She owned nearly the entire block, giving a portion of it for the city library, and she had elaborate gardens.

The Dunbars bought the house in October 1986 and opened their B&B the following June. Many original light fixtures, wallpaper and tile remain, as do original leaded glass windows, glass block walls in the kitchen and some of Sylvia Classon's furniture. The Dunbars are restoring the gardens, as well; Earl has 500 daffodils blooming in the spring. They want to replace the trellises found in historic photographs and host garden weddings.

Local wine and appetizers are served when guests arrive. Penny serves almost exclusively Wisconsin food. Guests can use the living areas downstairs and the TV and game room on the second floor.

Rooms and Rates: Four - All upstairs. Greenwood Room has queen brass bed, private half bath - $50. Windsor Room has queen canopy bed, sitting area, done in rose and grey with white lace - $65. Pine Room has pine paneling on one wall, antique oak double bed, mallard theme wallpaper - $45. Garden Room has queen pewter bed and day bed, window seat, overlooks the garden, done in blues - $50. Windsor, Pine and Garden rooms share bath with whirlpool with shower. Each additional person, $5. Add tax.

Meals: Breakfast is served in the dining room at a time arranged the night before. It may include homemade muffins or fruit coffeecake and a main entree, such as Wisconsin cheese and potato scrambled eggs, or ham, broccoli and cheese strata.

Dates open: Year 'round

Smoking: No

Children: Over 12

Pets: "Dachshund on premises"

Nearby: Lake Michigan beach, 3 blocks. Fishing, a lighthouse, jail museum, historic courthouse square, local artists, library, all within walking or biking distance. Grandfather clock and furniture factory outlet, 1 mile. Car ferry crosses to Ludington, Mich., 1.5 miles. X-c and downhill skiing, sledding, skating, 3 miles. Breummer County Park (small zoo), 3 miles.

Location/Directions: From Highway 29 east to Kewaunee, turn right on Highway 42 (Milwaukee Street) up hill to Rose Street, by Marquette Middle School. Turn right; inn is on corner of Dodge and Rose. Chicago, 3.5 hours. Madison, 3.5 hours. Milwaukee, 2.5 hours. Twin Cities, 6.5 hours.

Deposit: First night's lodging

Payment: Cash, personal or traveler's checks only

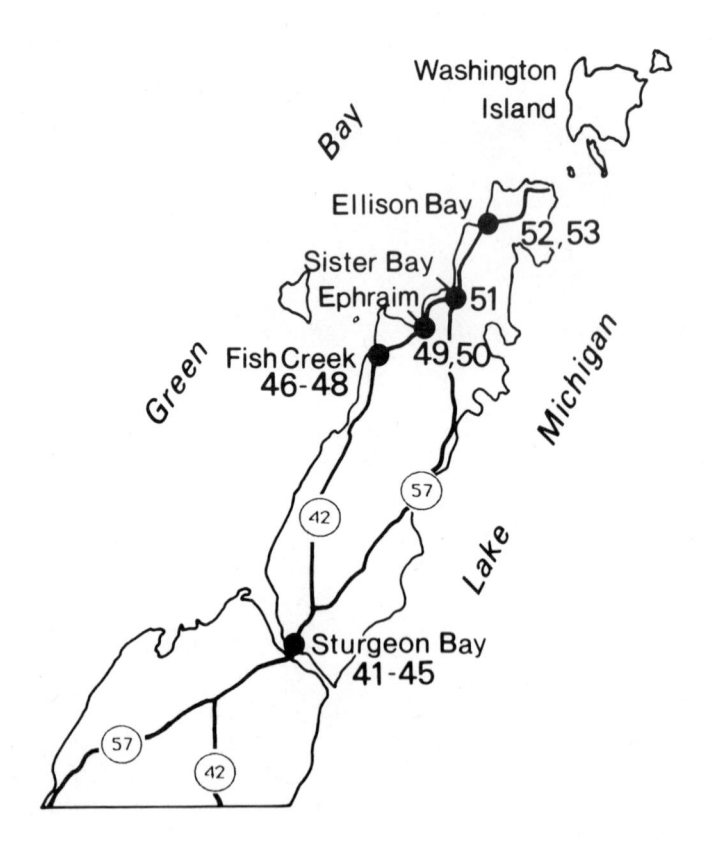

-Door County
41. The Barbican - Sturgeon Bay..................................114-115
42. Bay Shore Inn - Sturgeon Bay................................116-117
43. The Inn at Cedar Crossing - Sturgeon Bay..............118-119
44. The Scofield House - Sturgeon Bay........................120-121
45. The White Lace Inn - Sturgeon Bay........................122-123
46. Thorp House Inn - Fish Creek................................124-125
47. The Whistling Swan - Fish Creek...........................126-127
48. The White Gull Inn - Fish Creek............................128-129
49. The French Country Inn - Ephraim........................130-131
50. The Hillside Hotel - Ephraim..................................132-133
51. The Renaissance Inn - Sister Bay..........................134-135
52. The Griffin Inn - Ellison Bay..................................136-137
53. The Nelson Farm - Ellison Bay..............................138-139

Sturgeon Bay

The Barbican

132 N. Second Ave.
Sturgeon Bay, WI 54235
414-743-4854

Owner/Operator:
Jim Pichette

For years The Barbican was known as "the Gaede House" for one of its first owners, and as an antique and jewelry store, but this B&B is really going into its second era as a guest house.

Built over four years from 1907-1911, the house was a wedding present for Ruth Emily Gaede, the daughter of Ruth and L.M. Washburn, whose lumber yard was across the street. It was "the Gaede House" until Ruth Gaede's son sold the property in 1947. For about 25 years, the home then housed boarders, some from the Navy shipyards, some who stayed at "Second Avenue Tourist Home." In 1974, it was converted to an antique shop, then a jewelry store. Years later, the home was purchased with the idea of a B&B in mind.

But not by Jim Pichette. Pichette wanted it, but another buyer got there first. When the buyer rented the house instead of converting it to a B&B, Pichette found himself still obsessed with the idea, so he made an offer. Pichette's family is from the area, and his brother and sister-in-law, Mike and Cherrie Pichette, own the carpet business in an historic home next door. "The idea is to use the carriage house and Mike and Cherrie's house and make it into a little complex," he said.

Redoing just this one home has been no small project. The Pichettes worked on it themselves, "non-stop for four-and-a-half months." All the woodwork was taken off, walls papered and painted, and the woodwork put back on. Leaded glass windows and lace curtains are found throughout the home.

Guests are welcome to use the common room downstairs.

Rooms and Rates: Four - All queen beds, private baths and king-sized whirlpools. Bridgeview Suite is upstairs, black iron bed, sitting area, done in mauve and green, bath with separate shower - $75. Grandma's Room has gas fireplace, bath with tub and shower, coach and TV, done in lilac and burgundy - $105. Cottage Suite has sitting room downstairs with refrigerator, stereo, TV and whirlpool, upstairs is bedroom, bath with tub and shower, private terrace - $110. Library Suite is in the former library and dining room, whirlpool is under wood canopy, bed curtain, fireplace, stereo, TV refrigerator, bath with tub and shower, done in dark burgundy - $110. Rates are singles or doubles; no triples. Two-night minimum weekends; three-night minimum holiday weekends. Add tax.

Meals: Breakfast is served at a time arranged the night before and served in the dining room or to rooms. It may include a vareity of muffins, breads and coffeecakes and a fruit bowl.

Dates open: Year 'round   **Smoking:** Yes

Children: Yes (in separate room)   **Pets:** No

Nearby: Shops, restaurants, Door County Museum and Library, Miller Art Center, historic districts, community square, parks, beach, excursion boat, all downtown or within walking distance. Potowatomi State Park, 3 miles. Whitefish Dunes and Cave Point, 12 miles. Groomed x-c trails.

Location/Directions: Take Highway 42/57 across bridge, turn right on N. Second. Inn is two blocks away on the right. Chicago, 4.5 hours. Madison, 3.5 hours. Milwaukee, 3 hours. Twin Cities, 7 hours.

Deposit: First night's lodging

Payment: Cash, personal or traveler's checks, VISA or MasterCard

Sturgeon Bay

Bay Shore Inn

4205 Bay Shore Dr.
Sturgeon Bay, WI 54235
414-743-4551

Owners: Betty Hanson,
   son John Hanson, Paul Mathias
Managers: Susan and Paul Mathias

Jacob Hanson was one of many Norwegians who was reminded of his homeland and settled in Door County in the mid 1800s because of that. A sailing captain, he lived with his wife, Suzanna, and father.

The steamers and, later, trains brought summer tourists from St. Louis and Chicago who were seeking relief from summer heat by the Lake Michigan shore. Since they were always looking for a place to take meals or stay, Suzanna and a neighbor began serving summer boarders. Suzanna and Jacob's daughter-in-law, Matilda, was sometimes asked to come to help with the visitors.

In 1921, Matilda and John converted a former barn, used for the family's apple and cherry orchards, into a "Main Lodge." A lobby, dining room and kitchen were on the first floor, with guest rooms on the second.

This second generation of Hansons raised five children, and two of them, Elizabeth and Sanford (whom everyone knows as "Duke"), carried on the family business from the 1940s as the Bay Shore Inn.

Now the Inn is in the third and fourth generation of Hanson ownership. Duke died in 1985, to the sorrow of guests who knew him well. "It was his life, it really was," said Susan Mathias. Duke was very involved with the business, from orchestrating the traditional Door County fish boils to overseeing its expansion from one lodge to a complete resort with cottages and several other separate housing units.

The resort continues its traditions of Swedish cooking and family recreation. Guests have use of the beach, tennis courts and an indoor recreation center, and can swim, sail, hike, fish, bike or play lawn games.

In addition to the Main Lodge, the other historic structure on the property is the home in which the Hanson family once lived. It is now rented out as the Early American House, which has three units.

Rooms and Rates: Nine in Main Lodge - Bay or courtyard view, double or double and twin wicker beds, private bath with shower only, air conditioned, electric heat and cable TV. All have country wallpaper. Big screen TV/sitting room at the end of hall. $45 single, $90 double. Each additional person, $25. Add tax. Weekly and off-season rates. Three units - Early American House, same rates.

Meals: Continental breakfast included in room rates weekdays, May to June 12 and in September and October. Restaurant serves breakfast and dinner daily June 13-Aug. 25. Lunch can be made in a picnic basket and taken out. Modified American Plan offered in July and August. Traditional Door County fish boil prepared and served on beach.

Dates open: Year 'round   **Smoking:** Yes

Children: Yes   **Pets:** No

Nearby: Swimming, boating, tennis, sailing, recreation building, nature trail, bicyles at the resort. Golf, horseback riding in area.

Location/Directions: From Highway 42/57, cross the bridge and turn left on First Street. Take it until it runs into N. Third, which is Bay Shore Drive. Inn is on the left in about 2.5 miles. Chicago, 4.5 hours. Madison, 3.5 hours. Milwaukee, 3 hours. Twin Cities, 7 hours.

Deposit: 25 percent

Payment: Cash, personal or traveler's checks, VISA, MasterCard or Discover

Sturgeon Bay

The Inn at Cedar Crossing
336 Louisiana
Sturgeon Bay, WI 54235
414-743-4200

Owner/Operator:
Terry Wulf

Across the country, there were thousands of them -- downtown buildings modeled after European markets in which the merchants had their store at street level and lived upstairs. One of Sturgeon Bay's historic districts is no exception.

Located on the corner of Louisiana and Third is such a building. Since 1884, the stores in this building have included a pharmacy, a boutique and, in the 1930s, Miller's Clothing. That store belonged to the father of Gerhard Miller, considered the granddaddy of Door County artists, and young Gerhard worked in the store. He passed it on to his son, David, who operates it today in the shop next door.

In 1985, a number of factors brought the building (offices and apartments at the time) and Terry Wulf together. Wulf, a banker with a finance and marketing background, was "itching to get out" and into a business of her own. Being a supporter of downtown renovation, she was aware the building was available and had an idea of what it could become: an inn like those she had stayed in in the French Quarter of Quebec and heard about in Europe, which were located above shops in downtowns.

Wulf bought the building in December 1985. The upstairs apartments were removed and nine guest rooms and a parlor with fireplace were put in. All the plumbing, electricity, heating and air conditioning were redone or added. Wulf herself decorated each room differently. Downstairs, in the lobby/entrance off Louisiana Street, the original tin ceiling remains. The building is listed on the National Register of Historic Places.

After seven months, the inn opened Memorial Day weekend 1986. "I still have bags under my eyes," Wulf jokes. But guests are not likely to have any. Details are important, down to hand-dipped chocolates placed in rooms at night.

Rooms and Rates: Nine - All upstairs in country decor with antiques, private baths with tubs and showers, down pillows and comforters and air conditioners. Rates $54-84. Examples include: #2, queen four-poster bed, stenciled walls, done in lilac - $54. #6, sitting area, queen bed, done in greens - $74. # 7, Anniversary Room has king brass canopy bed, ivory lace curtains, king-sized whirlpool with separate shower - $84. #8 has canopy bed, stenciled walls and private sun deck - $59. Rates are double; singles $7 less. Each additional person, $7. Add tax. Extended stay discounts November through April.

Meals: Continental breakfast is served 8-10 in the restaurant on the first floor. It includes fresh fruit and homemade muffins, granola, sugar cakes or nut breads. The restaurant is open to the public 11:30-2:30 Monday-Saturday for lunch.

Dates open: Year 'round   **Smoking:** Not encouraged

Children: Talk with innkeeper   **Pets:** No

Nearby: Shops, restaurants, Door County Museum and Library, Miller Art Center, historic districts, community square, parks, beach, excursion boat, all downtown or within walking distance. Potowatomi State Park, 3.5 miles. Whitefish Dunes and Cave Point, 12 miles. Groomed x-c ski trails.

Location/Directions: Located downtown on the corner of Louisiana and Third streets. Entrance is on Louisiana; the front of the building has ice cream parlor and candy shop. Chicago, 4.5 hours. Madison, 3.5 hours. Milwaukee, 3 hours. Twin Cities, 7 hours.

Deposit: First night's lodging

Payment: Cash, personal or traveler's checks, VISA, MasterCard or Discover

Sturgeon Bay

The Scofield House
908 Michigan
Sturgeon Bay, WI 54235
414-743-7727

Owners/Operators:
Fran and Bill Cecil

Herbert Scofield at one time owned what was believed to be Wisconsin's largest hardware store, so it's no wonder that his home contained the finest that his considerable connections with the construction trade could buy.

The carved and inlaid woodwork, which features intricate faces and patterns, has been kept in good condition over the 86 years since the home was built, owners Fran and Bill Cecil found. The ornate oak stretches throughout the first floor, including the ceiling, and up the stairs. The leaded glass is not just any glass, but crystal, and there are five types of wood in the inlaid borders of the hardwood floors.

As fourth owners of the home, the Cecils found the large single-family home needed a good deal of work before it could be opened as a B&B. For example, the floors were sanded, each room was wallpapered, ceiling fans were installed, and the home was rewired. Outside, the colors of paint chosen were from an 1887 paint company sample book. "It took 10 days in the Valspar labs in Minneapolis to match it," then the house absorbed 68 gallons of the stuff, said Bill.

Both Fran and Bill were Milwaukee health care executives who decided on a career change to innkeeping. With a penchant for travel, Victorian-era restoration and entertaining, opening a B&B "seemed a natural extension of our interests," Bill said. Besides, Bill had worked with Jim Roberts, of the Griffin Inn in Ellison Bay, who had left the health care field to take up innkeeping with Laurie, his wife. "Seeing how very happy they were had a a very strong influence," Bill said.

Guests are welcome to use the dining and living rooms downstairs, the 1880 upright piano in the parlor, the telescope and the gazebo. Fran's wholewheat chocolate chip cookies are always available.

Rooms and Rates: Four - All upstairs, all share two baths with tub and shower. Rose Room has double antique walnut bed, parquet floor, done in rose and cream - $52. Blue Room has ruffled curtains, walnut bed, cedar floor, family heirloom antique quilt and furniture - $52. Wicker Room is the former maid's room, is carpeted, has white iron and brass queen bed, done in floral pattern of black, rose, green and white - $52. Suite has double bed with crocheted lace spread, own sitting room, balcony over front porch - $55. Rates are doubles; $47 singles. No triples. Two-night minimum stay on weekends; three-night on holiday weekends. Add tax. Ski packages and off-season discounts.

Meals: Breakfast is served buffet-style or in a basket to the rooms 8-10. It includes fresh mixed fruit with a peach schnapps marinade, honey bran cherry nut muffins, and an omelette, Welsh rarebit, fried scrapple or a casserole of sausage, mushrooms, cheese and sour cream, or whatever else Bill decides to cook.

Dates open: Year 'round   **Smoking:** No

Children: Over 14   **Pets:** No

Nearby: Shops, restaurants, Door County Museum and Library, Miller Art Center, historic districts, community square, parks, beach, excursion boat, all downtown or within walking distance. Potowatami State Park, 3.5 miles. Whitefish Dunes and Cave Point, 12 miles. Groomed x-c ski trails.

Location/Directions: Take Business 42/57 over bridge; it becomes Michigan Street. Follow to corner of Ninth. Chicago, 4.5 hours. Madison, 3.5 hours. Milwaukee, 3 hours. Twin Cities, 7 hours.

Deposit: Half of room rate

Payment: Cash, personal or traveler's checks only

Sturgeon Bay

The White Lace Inn

16 N. Fifth St.
Sturgeon Bay, WI 54235
414-743-1105

Owners/Operators:
Bonnie and Dennis Statz

In 1903, a Victorian home was built by Sturgeon Bay lawyer Richard Cody (a distant relative of Buffalo Bill) and Sadie, his wife. Sadie outlived her husband by some 40 years, living there until her death in 1948. Then the house was used as a meeting hall.

"When we saw it in 1981, the Knights of Columbus were meeting here, the Girl Scouts, there were prom dinners," said Dennis Statz. No one lived in it and heavy green drapes covered the windows. "From 1908 to 1982, the lights had very seldom been on."

Dennis and Bonnie have changed all that. When they decided to go into business, they looked at possible inns in New England and Michigan before deciding on Sturgeon Bay. They bought the house in April 1982 and opened as an inn in July after rewiring, replumbing, redecorating and extensive restoration, down to replacing the narrow wood siding. The second floor, which was one big meeting room, was rebuilt into guest rooms.

But the story doesn't stop there. In 1983, an 1880s house in town was about to be razed for a bank building, so the Statzs had it moved to their large lot. Again, after major renovation and restoration, the Garden House opened as part of the White Lace Inn.

Then a house adjacent to theirs came up for sale. It had been owned by the Washburn family; the Prange Department Store in town was once the Prange-Washburn Department Store. For the third time, the Statzs repeated their renovation work.

Linens and the decor give the White Lace Inn a romantic look, and the Statzs have been witnesses at several weddings (there will be more as the garden is expanded). Guests may gather in the main house for games, TV or a fire in the parlor fireplace.

Meals: Continental breakfast is served in the Main House dining room or by the fireplace in the parlor from 8-10. It includes Scandinavian fruit soup (hot in winter, cold in summer), banana and zucchini breads or hot homebaked banana and bran muffins.

Rooms and Rates: 15 in three houses - All with private baths and air conditioning, 10 with fireplaces, four with whirlpools. In Main House, five, $55-70. In Garden House, six, each with fireplace, $65-78. In Washburn House, four, two of which are suites. Each room has double raised whirlpool, fireplace, queen bed, stereo, TV and down comforter. Rooms A, C or D are $98. Room B has sitting room, two-sided fireplace, Eastlake bed with matching dresser, white lace and peach decor, raised double whirlpool and separate shower - $120. Rates are doubles; singles $7 less. Two or three night minimums required some weekends. Add tax.

Dates open: Year 'round   **Smoking:** Some no-smoking rooms

Children: Not for young children   **Pets:** No

Nearby: Shops, restaurants, Door County Museum and Library, Miller Art Center, historic districts, community square, parks, beach, excursion boat, all downtown or within walking distance. Potowatomi State Park, 3.5 miles. Whitefish Dunes and Cave Point, 12 miles. Groomed x-c ski trails.

Location/Directions: Take Business 42/57 over bridge, and it turns into Michigan Street. Follow it to Fifth, turn left. The inn is on the right. Map sent. Chicago, 4.5 hours. Madison, 3.5 hours. Milwaukee, 3 hours. Twin Cities, 7 hours.

Deposit: First night's lodging

Payment: Cash, personal or traveler's checks, VISA or MasterCard

Fish Creek

Thorp House Inn

4135 Bluff Rd.
P.O. Box 90R
Fish Creek, WI 54212
414-868-2444

Owners/Operators:
Christine and Sverre Falck-Pedersen

Asa Thorp, founder of Fish Creek, was granted land from President James Buchanan in 1858 to build a dock for steamers, which bought the wood he sold to fire their boilers. In 1902, his nephew, Freeman Thorp, and Jessie, his wife, began building their Victorian home on the hillside. But on Oct. 3, 1903, Freeman Thorp died when the steamer Erie L. Hackley went down on Green Bay, taking 11 people with her. He was on the way back from across the bay, getting lumber for their new home.

Knowing that she would have to support herself, Jessie continued construction and then ran a boarding house. Then other women became innkeepers of sorts. Julie Anderson-Hansen added three cottages, offered homecooking in the main house and called the place Cedar Ridge Lodge. Ida Anderson bought it in the 1940s, built three more cottages and called her boarding house Breezy Hill Lodge, running it into the 1960s. Sally and Pat Kinsey, a nephew of Jessie Thorp, also ran the cottages. Finally, for three summers it housed summer help for a nearby restaurant.

That's when Chris and Sverre Falck-Pedersen found it, full of modern furniture and lighting and in need of restoration and renovation. Living south of Chicago at the time, Chris was a cosmetics sales rep, Sverre a metallurical engineer. "Our interests were in renovation, antiques and entertaining, so our avocation turned into our vocation and we changed professions," Sverre said. They bought the house and cottages in February 1986.

Four guest rooms were open the following August. Much of the refinishing, carpentry, painting and wallpapering was done by themselves. Chris did the decorating, settling on antiques, lace curtains and embroidered sheets and pillow cases.

Guests are welcome to use the summer porch and the downstairs parlor with original stone fireplace.

Meals: Continental breakfast is served in the kitchen from 8-10 and may include fresh fruit, homemade currant scones and muffins, such as apricot-filled or blueberry.

Rooms and Rates: Four - All upstairs with ceiling fans and individual thermostats. Rooms share two full baths, one with clawfoot tub and shower, other with shower only. Maria Claflin Room has queen pine bed with hand-tied net canopy, embroidered comforter, view of the bay - $58. Jessie Kinsey Thorp Room has triple windows facing the harbor, 8-foot high walnut double bed - $58. Lillian Thorp Room has double bed with head set back into an arched alcove - $53. Emma Thorp Room rented only as suite with Lillian Thorp Room. It has sleeper sofa and is done in grey and rose - $78 for three. Maid's Quarters is small room with double white iron double brass bed - $45. Rates are doubles; singles subtract $5. No triples (except suite). Add tax.

Dates open: Year 'round   **Smoking:** Not in guest rooms

Children: "Sorry, no"   **Pets:** No

Nearby: Peninsula State Park (beaches, picnic, bike, hike, golf, x-c skiing), 4 blocks. Marina, boat launch and excursion boats (sunset cruises), beach, 2 blocks. Founder's Square shops and restaurants, 2 blocks. Peninsula Players summer stock, 1.5 miles. Music festivals, classical music concerts, art galleries.

Location/Directions: From Highway 42, turn right on Bluff Road one block before Main Street. House is on right side of road. Map provided. Chicago, 5 hours. Madison, 4 hours. Milwaukee, 3.5 hours. Twin Cities, 7.5 hours.

Deposit: First night's lodging

Payment: Cash, personal or traveler's checks only

Fish Creek

The Whistling Swan

P.O. Box 193
Fish Creek, WI 54212
414-868-3442

Owners/Operators:
Jan and Andy Coulson
Manager: Jan Coulson

Dr. Herman Welcker was a determined man. When the virologist from Milwaukee settled in Fish Creek, he was eager to get into the resort business in a big way. He arrived in 1896 and began buying and building inns and cottages.

After the turn-of-the-century, he took a fancy to a club house in Marinette, known as "the Chicago and Northeastern Eating House." He purchased the building, which had been built in 1887. Welcker had it dismantled, rolled on logs pulled by horses across the frozen Green Bay, and rebuilt in Fish Creek. He added gaming tables for his male guests and called it "Dr. Welcker's Casino."

Today it's The Whistling Swan. The shop and reservation desk on the main floor were Welcker's lobby and game rooms. One of the original gaming tables, with shelves for drinks or poker chips, is in the foyer, as is the baby grand piano on which Henriette Welcker played for guests.

Jan and Andy Coulson bought the inn (then called Proud Mary) in November 1985, after purchasing the White Gull Inn (other parts of Welcker's resort properties) in 1972. They began renovation and didn't open until June 1986. Fourteen original bedrooms on the second floor with shared baths were changed to seven, three of which are suites. The foyer has been returned to its original, larger size. The inn also had to be painted, papered, and have new electrical, plumbing, heating and air conditioning systems. And the wavy floors were straightened.

Jan Coulson often is on duty in her shop on the first floor. Rooms are decorated in antiques or reproductions. Complimentary mineral water and, in the summer, fresh flowers are placed in each room. Downstairs, guests may use the foyer and the long dining porch in the afternoons for reading, playing card games, or people-watching.

Rooms and Rates: Seven - All on second floor with air conditioning, carpet, private baths with tub (five with clawfoot) and shower. Rooms 1, 2, 4 and 6 have double bed; example is #2, standard room with carved walnut bed, done in purple floral wallpaper - $70. Suites 3 and 5 have sitting area with sleeper sofa, separated with French doors, queen bed - $96. Room 7 has sleeper sofa, queen bed - $90. Rates are doubles or singles. Each additional person, $10. Two-night minimum on weekends; three nights on holiday weekends. Add tax. Extended stay discount.

Meals: Summer and fall rates include a continental breakfast served on the porch from 8-9:30. It may include fresh-squeezed juice, fresh fruit and baked goods, such as homemade granola, fresh-baked croissants and muffins. A full breakfast is included November through April, served at the White Gull Inn, 1 block away.

Dates open: Daily May-October and Christmas week; weekends rest of the year

Smoking: Not encouraged   **Children:** Yes   **Pets:** No

Nearby: Shops on premises. Peninsula State Park (beaches, picnic, bike, hike, golf, x-c skiing), 6 blocks. Marina, boat launch and excursion boats (sunset cruises), beach, 1-3 blocks. Founder's Square shops and restaurants, across the street. Peninsula Players summer stock, 1.5 miles. Music festivals, classical music concerts, art galleries. Sunset Park, 1 block.

Location/Directions: From Highway 42, come into town and turn left at the stop sign, then watch for the Whistling Swan on the right in about a block. Chicago, 5 hours. Madison, 4 hours. Milwaukee, 3.5 hours. Twin Cities, 7.5 hours.

Deposit: First night's lodging

Payment: Cash, personal or traveler's checks, VISA, MasterCard or AMEX

Fish Creek

The White Gull Inn

P.O. Box 159
Fish Creek, WI 54212
414-868-3517

Owners/Operators:
Jan and Andy Coulson
Manager: Joan Holliday

Dr. Herman Welcker is something of a legend in Fish Creek. A virologist from Milwaukee, he gave up medicine and moved to Fish Creek to make a name for himself in the tourism business.

He ended up owning several buildings as part of his substantial resort property. One, a large cottage built in 1896, he named after his wife, "The Henriette." Guests, arriving by steamer, were charged $7.50 a week.

In 1972, the Coulsons bought it. Their White Gull Inn has had several owners in between, but it always operated as a resort since it was "The Henriette" and is said to be the oldest continuously operating hotel in Door County.

Jan and Andy Coulson met while working summer jobs at the White Gull. They've tried to reunite many of Welcker's original resort buildings under their ownership. In addition to the "Lodge" with 10 rooms, they also have the Cliffhouse with four rooms, three cottages and the Lundberg House, one block from the Lodge. The cottages have fireplaces and are done in antiques. Beachcomber and Stowaway Cottages each have three bedrooms; Henrietta Cottage has two. The Lundberg House, built by the family who had the general store in town, has four bedrooms. All are rented to one party per cottage.

The Lodge itself has the same floor plan and verandas as in earlier days, but underwent a major renovation in the early 1980s. Rooms have antiques, wood, wicker or iron and brass furnishings. Downstairs, the lobby and dining rooms have hand-stenciling and decor which has been featured in Country Living Magazine.

Rooms and Rates: Ten - All with antique beds, some with sinks in room; three on first floor with private entrances and bathrooms. Rates $40 (twin bed only) - $80, double or single. #8 has private bath with shower, double bed, front balcony access, is on the second floor - $66. #9 has antique wood bed, lace curtains, rose print wallpaper, access to front balcony, shares two baths down the hall with showers only - $58. Cliffhouse has four rooms, all with air conditioning, carpet, TV and fireplace, and private bath. Rooms A and B on first floor, double bed, sleeper sofa - $95. Rooms C and D on second floor, smaller, $85. Rates are double or single. Two-night minimum on weekends; three nights on holiday weekends. Add tax. Rates slightly higher Nov. 1-April 30 because full breakfast is included. Extended stay and midweek package discounts in winter.

Meals: Breakfast included November through April. It is served in the restaurant and is ordered from the menu. The restaurant on the premises serves three meals a day to the public. Traditional Door County fish boil also served on selected nights year 'round.

Dates open: Year 'round

Smoking: Yes

Children: Yes

Pets: No

Nearby: Peninsula State Park (beaches, picnic, bike, hike, golf, x-c skiing), 7 blocks. Marina, boat launch and excursion boats (sunset cruises), beach, 1-3 blocks. Founder's Square shops and restaurants, 1 blocks. Peninsula Players summer stock, 1.5 miles. Music festivals, classical music concerts, art galleries.

Location/Directions: From Highway 42, turn left at the bottom of the hill in Fish Creek, following signs to Sunset Park. Inn is about two blocks on the left before the park. Chicago, 5 hours. Madison, 4 hours. Milwaukee, 3.5 hours. Twin Cities, 7.5 hours.

Deposit: First night's lodging

Payment: Cash, personal or traveler's checks, VISA, MasterCard or AMEX

Ephraim

The French Country Inn
30 Spruce Lane
Ephraim, WI 54211
414-854-4001

Owners/Operators:
Sandi and Bob Ball

Sandi and Bob Ball took their first trip to Door County in August 1986. On their second trip, two months later, they saw this inn, bought it, and moved in.

These people have no trouble making big decisions. "We both worked for other people," said Sandi. "We'd been talking about trying to get into something a little more relaxed." Based on those and other factors, like liking people and being from small towns, they made a major career change on the spot.

They're still gathering the history of the inn, but they know that when it was built in 1929, it was the main summer house for an estate that stretched to the Green Bay shoreline in front and about a block back from water's edge. In the 1930s, it was sold to an adjacent hotel, and the Kahler family bought it in the 1940s. Mrs. Kahler ran it as a boarding house, calling it "The Shelter," and filling it with overflow business from area hotels and inns.

The Kahler family passed it down through the years until 1984, when Marianne and Don Rechts bought it. They turned The Shelter into the French Country Inn. They are responsible for much of the inn's renovation.

The house is an atypical B&B, in that its design is much more like an old hunting lodge than a Victorian mansion. Local craftsmen built a huge fireplace downstairs out of stones from the beach. Walls and ceilings are of an extinct carved wallboard. Originally, the first floor stretched up into an open loft on the second floor. That has since been filled in, but guests can imagine the open area.

The Balls also rent one housekeeping cabin, which was the original ice house. Guests are free to use the grounds and the downstairs living room and fireplace. The sun porch, also open for guests, has original wicker furniture.

Rooms and Rates: Six (four in winter) - Rooms #1 and #2 are on first floor, rest on second. All rooms except #2 have large shared bath on second floor with tub and shower. Examples include: Room #2 has twin beds, view of harbor, private bath - $55. Room #3 has twin beds, done in beige, white and light blue, view of garden - $50. Room #5 has birdseye maple double bed, lace curtains, French doors open to sun porch, done in greens and white - $55. Rates are double or single; no triples. Add tax. The Cabin has main living room with fireplace, kitchen, bath with shower only, two bedrooms - $65 for no more than 4 adults.

Meals: Continental breakfast is served 8-10 in common area on first floor and includes fresh fruit, and croissants.

Dates open: Year 'round   **Smoking:** Not in guest rooms

Children: "Not recommended"   **Pets:** No

Nearby: Shopping, fishing and charters, restaurants all within walking distance. Sail, pontoon, windsurf, paddleboat rentals, 2 blocks. Anderson Store museum, 2 blocks. Peninsula State Park (beaches, picnic, bike, hike, golf, x-c skiing), half-mile.

Location/Directions: Take Highway 42 into Ephraim and turn onto Spruce Lane by the Edgewater Motel. Inn is half-block on the left. Chicago, 5 hours. Madison, 4 hours. Milwaukee, 3.5 hours. Twin Cities, 7.5 hours.

Deposit: First night's lodging

Payment: Cash, personal or traveler's checks only

Ephraim

The Hillside Hotel

9980 Water St.
P.O. Box 17
Ephraim, WI 54211
414-743-4551
Outside Wisconsin: 800-423-7023

Owners/Operators:
Evadne and Dean McNeil
Innkeepers:
Karen and David McNeil

When Moravian minister Andrew Iverson founded Ephraim in 1853, he built a two-room cobbler shop and residence on the hillside overlooking the waterfront. Within 10 years, Iverson had been asked to leave the socialistic community, and the Olson family bought the cobbler's shop from the church. "Grandpa" Olson, a steamship booking agent, became the link for Scandinavian immigrants. He could arrange passage by steamer to New York, rail to Chicago, and steamer to Ephraim.

As the Olson family grew, so did the house/shop. To pay for the additions, Serena "Grandma" Olson took in boarders. Ephraim became a popular place to get away from hay fever. For three generations, the Olson family lived here and ran what grew from two rooms to a hotel with a 96-foot veranda.

In 1969, Evadne and Dean McNeil were sailing and vacationing in the area with their four children, as they had for years, and they saw the "for sale" sign. When Dean, a dentist, came into the hotel's office, pulled a chair up to the window with waterfront view and let out a sigh of major proportions, Eve knew the hotel would be theirs. "He saw the view and I saw the work," she says, recalling the roof's holes and falling sand-and-horsehair plaster (preserved where possible).

The 1970s saw a boom in tourism for Door County. Tourists "would stay anyplace that would have them. People would come up on a bus and get off at 7 p.m. with no reservations," Eve recalled. The idea of preserving the historic hotel and having a viable business has kept the McNeil family at the Hillside Hotel since then, Eve earning both a master's and Ph.D. in summers here. In 1983, son David and daughter-in-law Karen signed on as innkeepers, winterized the place, opened it year 'round and added dinner service.

Guests can use the long porch, the private dock and the old piano in the music room. Cookies and hot cider and coffee are always available.

Meals: Breakfast is served at "promptly at 8 a.m." (alarm clocks available upon request) in the dining room. Entrees vary daily and may include Eggs Benedict, spinach and bacon quiche and muffins, or fresh, local smoked whitefish with broccoli and Bearnaise sauce. Dinners are served year 'round by reservation only.

Rooms and Rates: 12 - All on second floor with shared baths. Iron beds, handmade quilts. Two full baths on second floor have clawfoot tubs and showers; downstairs one shower room and one half-bath available. All carpeted except #10 and #11, which are adjoining rooms above the original two rooms of the hotel and have pine plank floors, rag rugs, lace curtains and red wallpaper. $45 single, $57 double. Add tax. Two-night minimums on holiday/special event weekends. Two cottages on the premises are rented by the week or two-night minimums of $95 per night for up to six persons, $75 up to four.

Dates open: May 1 - Nov. 1; Dec. 29 - March 1   **Pets:** No

Children: Yes (separate room often necessary)   **Smoking:** On porches only

Nearby: Private beach with swimming, dock and small boat mooring, across the street. Shopping, fishing and charters, restaurants all within walking distance. Sail, pontoon, windsurf, paddleboat rentals, 1 block. Anderson Store museum, 5 blocks. Peninsula State Park (beaches, picnic, bike, hike, golf, x-c skiing), half-mile. Tennis courts, 1 block.

Location/Directions: Inn is on Highway 42, two doors south of Willson's ice cream parlor. Chicago, 5 hours. Madison, 4 hours. Milwaukee, 3.5 hours. Twin Cities, 7.5 hours.

Deposit: For one night stays, entire amount; half of room rate for extended stays

Payment: Cash, personal or traveler's checks, VISA, MasterCard or AMEX

Sister Bay

The Renaissance Inn
414 Maple Dr.
Sister Bay, WI 54234
414-854-5107

Owners/Operators:
JoDee and John Faller

From the street, this B&B inn must look much the same way as when it was built about 1893, with a storefront downstairs. There's hardly an idea that five guestrooms would be located upstairs.

Over the years, the building has had many purposes that befit its Door County surroundings: a bait store, an ice cream parlor, a grocery store, a store that sold stoves, a boarding house, and a butcher shop and well-known sausage factory. No doubt that has been at least partly due to its central location, just down a sidestreet from Highway 42 in downtown Sister Bay.

The Fallers bought the inn in 1983 and moved to Door County. John, a chef for 25 years, and JoDee, a department store buyer, wanted a change and a good opportunity for John to own and operate a small gourmet restaurant. Faller's Seafood Restaurant, located in the former storefront and porch downstairs, has been completely redecorated and serves local and other seafood, some of it Cajun-style, plus beef options.

Upstairs, JoDee runs a B&B because "it was something up and coming, and we really wanted to do it," JoDee said. The upstairs was gutted, and workers put in new plumbing, wiring and heating, then it was decorated with antiques. It took about four months of work and the B&B opened in July 1983.

The inn is on the National Register of Historic Places because it is built of stovewood, a unique way of building with round log inner walls, almost all of which are no longer visible. Quilts on the beds were handmade by JoDee's mother and sister.

One upstairs room serves as a parlor, where a TV and board games are for guests' use.

Rooms and Rates: Five - All upstairs with corner sinks, ceiling fans, carpet and air conditioners. Each has private bath with shower only. Examples include: #3 with antique double bed and twin with blue comforters; #6 with black iron double bed and lace curtains; #7 with high walnut bed and handmade quilt. $55 single or double. Room #3, 3 people, $70. Otherwise no triples. Two-night minimum during the summer; three nights on holiday weekends. Add tax. Winter packages.

Meals: Breakfast is served at 9 in the restaurant. It may include a fruit plate, home-baked breads and muffins, sausage and vegetable quiche or French toast or pancakes. Faller's Seafood Restaurant is on the premises and serves lunch in the summer and dinner year 'round.

Dates open: Closed Nov., Dec., mid-March to mid-April   **Smoking:** Yes

Children: Over 14 (in separate room)   **Pets:** No

Nearby: Municipal beach and downtown, 1 block. Golf course, half-mile. Biking and hiking.

Location/Directions: Take Highway 42 to Maple Drive (Bundas Department Store is on the corner), turn left. Inn is down the block on the right. Chicago, 5 hours. Madison, 4 hours. Milwaukee, 3.5 hours. Twin Cities, 7.5 hours.

Deposit: Half of room rate

Payment: Cash, personal or traveler's checks, VISA, MasterCard, AMEX or Discover

Ellison Bay

The Griffin Inn

11976 Mink River Rd.
Ellison Bay, WI 54210
414-854-4306

Owners/Operators:
Laurie and Jim Roberts

Laurie and Jim Roberts literally became innkeepers overnight. On March 13, 1986, they loaded the car with groceries in Milwaukee, drove to Door County to close the sale of the inn, and then began preparations for 10 guests arriving the next day and needing five meals to be served on a winter weekend. "Trial by fire," Laurie says, laughing now.

But the Roberts don't regret the decision to buy an established inn. Quite the contrary. They planned on eventually retiring to Door County, where Laurie spent all her summers as a child, and just speeded up the move by a good 25 years or so. "If we could have moved here when we retired," Laurie said, "I would've thought we had made it. We're just thrilled to be here now -- though we're a whole lot busier than we thought we'd be!"

The inn was built in 1910 as a private residence on 18 acres. In 1921, the two Wickman brothers switched houses, and Gilbert and Olga Wickman moved in to what they called the Ellison Bay Lodge. They added living room space and five rooms upstairs, eventually building cottages in back of the inn. It was theirs for 40 years.

Since the Wickmans sold it in the early 1960s, the inn changed hands, had absentee owners and shrunk to five acres of land. Jim, a hospital administrator, and Laurie, "a full-time mom and overextended volunteer," had decided to change priorities as their daughters were growing up. They looked for a business in Door County to buy and run together. Laurie's parents live in Fish Creek and "when my mom called and told us the Griffin Inn was for sale, we were up four hours later." Six weeks later they moved in.

The Roberts have redone the dining room and redecorated rooms. In the living room after dinner, guests get to talking around a big bowl of community popcorn. Guests may help themselves to coffee, tea or cocoa and use the two porch swings, the gazebo, the library and the living room with fireplace, and a refrigerator is available.

Meals: The breakfast bell is clanged at 8:30 and breakfast is served in the dining room. It may include Apple-Bacon-Cheddar Bake or Ham and Cheese Puff, brown sugar oatmeal muffins, poppyseed coffeecake and fresh fruit.

Rooms and Rates: Ten - All upstairs, carpeted, with antique beds and done in decor to match homemade quilts. They share two and a half-baths down the hall, one with shower, one with tub and shower. Examples include: #2, corner room with two windows, ruffled curtains, carved walnut double bed. #4 has white iron and brass double bed, done in white, blue and pink. $47 single, $52 double, $62 triple. Two night stays required for advance reservations. Add tax. Winter packages. Four cottages available, each sleeps four, has private bath with shower only, TV, refrigerator, done in rough cedar paneling. Breakfast basket is picked up in kitchen at 8:30. $58 double. Each additional person, $5.

Dates open: Year 'round

Smoking: Not in guest rooms

Children: Over 6 at the inn; all ages in cottages

Pets: No

Nearby: Sports court for tennis or basketball on grounds. Liberty Grove township park (beach, tennis, picnicking), art galleries, restaurants and shops, 1-4 blocks. Ferries to Washington Island, 7 miles. Newport State Park (beach, hiking and x-c skiing), 8 miles. Ellison Bluff County Park, 1.5 miles. Door Bluff Headlands County Park, 2 miles. The Clearing (adult education), 1 mile.

Location/Directions: From Highway 42, turn right in Ellison Bay on Mink River Road. Inn is two blocks ahead on the left. Chicago, 5.5 hours. Madison, 4.5 hours. Milwaukee, 4 hours. Twin Cities, 8 hours.

Deposit: Half of entire stay

Payment: Cash, personal or traveler's checks only

Ellison Bay

Nelson Farm

1526 Ranch Lane
Ellison Bay, WI 54210
414-854-5224

Owners/Operators:
June and John Nelson

June and John Nelson found this little 24-acre farm in 1983, when John retired from a supposed retirement. They owned a house in Sister Bay and called it retirement, but John still commuted to Chicago occasionally. The farm in Ellison Bay, just two blocks from Highway 42, was big enough to keep them busy, but small enough to claim they had really retired this time.

Andrew Wickman, a Swedish immigrant, settled the land with his family when he homesteaded in 1860. The 300 acres were handed down within the Wickman family until about 30 years ago.

The original 300 acres have since been sold in smaller parcels, and 40 have gone to the Nature Conservancy. On the Nelson's 24 acres, about half are woods and half are field. John and June do not farm in a big way, but have a bigger-than-average garden. They raise strawberries, blackberries and raspberries, plus vegetables, geese and chickens. Four horses are boarded in the barn, and there are usually two dogs and two cats around.

It was June Nelson's idea a few years after buying the farm in 1983 to open the B&B. She wanted to open a B&B at an easy, unhurried pace after reading about them for years. "I've never traveled that way but I've always wanted to," she said. "I've always been fascinated with them, but I had to convince my husband." After opening two bedrooms in 1987, "my husband is really enjoying it and now he's the one pushing me!"

Since they bought the farm and its seven buildings, the house has been completely redecorated, with new electrical work, and a wrap-around deck and large balcony added. Guests are also welcome to feed the chickens and collect eggs, which June says is a real treat for city folks who've never done that. The geese come honking right up to the fence to "talk" to visitors, and the horses look on as gentle giants. Guests also can walk in the woods, relax on the deck or use a TV placed upstairs.

Rooms and Rates: Two - Both upstairs, sharing bath with tub and shower, with some modern decor. Beige room has double bed, view of barns - $40. Blue room has two double beds and a crib, dormer roof - $45. Rates are singles or doubles. Each additional person, $5. Add tax.

Meals: Breakfast is served on the deck or in the dining room at about 8. It may include fresh seasonal fruit, such as strawberries or raspberries from the farm, homemade breads, coffeecake and jam, eggs from the farm and bacon, or apple pancakes, or omelettes.

Dates open: Year 'round   **Smoking:** No

Children: Yes   **Pets:** No

Nearby: Liberty Grove township park (beach, tennis, picnicking), art galleries, restaurants and shops, 4 blocks. Ferries to Washington Island, 7 miles. Newport State Park (beach, hiking and x-c skiing), 8 miles. Ellison Bluff County Park, 1.5 miles. Door Bluff Headlands County Park, 2 miles. The Clearing (adult education), 1 mile.

Location/Directions: Go through Ellison Bay on 47. Turn right on Lakeview Road by the blue Severson sign. Turn left in a half-block on Ranch Lane; farm is at end of road. Chicago, 5.5 hours. Madison, 4.5 hours. Milwaukee, 4 hours. Twin Cities, 8 hours.

Deposit: First night's lodging

Payment: Cash, personal or traveler's checks only

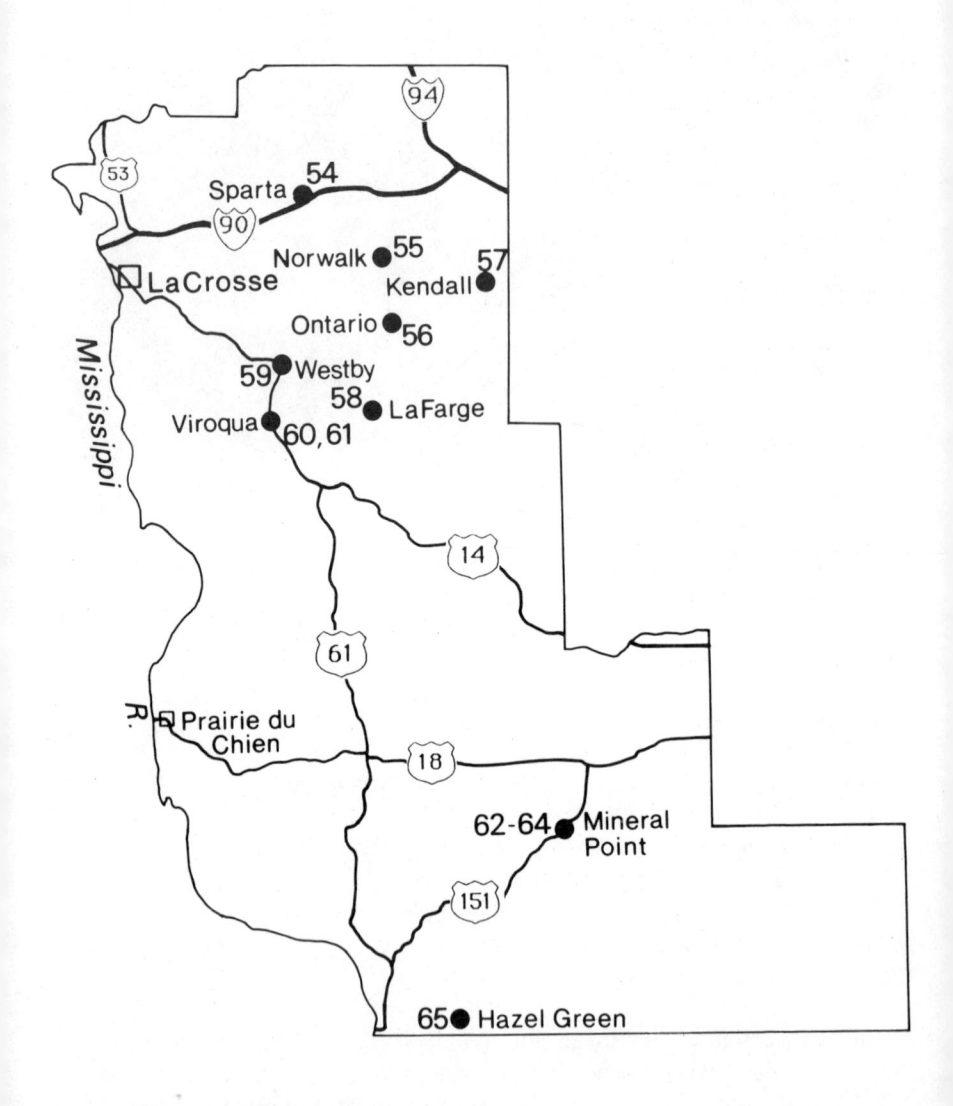

-Hidden Valleys

54. Just-N-Trails - Sparta 142-143
55. Lonesome Jake's Devil's Hole Ranch - Norwalk 144-145
56. Downings' B&B - Ontario 146-147
57. Dusk to Dawn B&B - Kendall 148-149
58. Trillium - LaFarge 150-151
59. Westby House - Westby 152-153
60. Serendipity Farm - Viroqua 154-155
61. Viroqua Heritage Inn - Viroqua 156-157
62. The Chesterfield Inn - Mineral Point 158-159
63. The Duke House - Mineral Point 160-161
64. The Jones House - Mineral Point 162-163
65. The Wisconsin House Stagecoach Inn - Hazel Green ... 164-165

Sparta

Just-N-Trails

Route 1, Box 263
Sparta, WI 54656
608-269-4522

Owners/Operators:
Donna and Don Justin

This neat-as-a-pin farm with requisite red barn has been in Don Justin's family since 1914. His grandfather, who also carved church altars in LaCrosse, had the house built in 1920 and there have been no major structural changes since then.

"His parents had taken very good care of the house," said Donna Justin, who, with Don, bought the farm in 1970. "Fortunately, they didn't throw very many things away." Two examples are the copper boiler now in the dining room, which was tucked away under the stairway, and the butternut dry sink, which was in the garage. Don and Donna did strip the home's natural woodwork and floor "and it took 18 gallons of Zip Strip," she revealed.

The dairy farm is home to about 50 cows. Donna milks and Don does the feeding and care of the animals, which guests can watch, Donna said. They also grow corn, alfalfa and oats.

Just-N-Trails opened as a private cross-country ski touring center in the winter of 1985 when the Justins looked to supplement their income. "We have 200 acres, but only 70 are tillable -- all that land with trees and hills, for recreation, is real attractive, but not for farming," she explained.

"Everything just fell into place" for the B&B, Donna said, which opened in October 1986. They had two extra bedrooms upstairs, the B&B industry was taking off and Donna was no longer teaching but working part-time.

B&B guests come to see the farm in the summer, hike and be in the woods in the spring and fall, and x-c ski in the winter -- and sometimes a little of each in overlapping seasons. The ski trails, named after deer which often are seen in the hills or on the edge of the cornfields, make good summer hiking trails. In the winter, guests park their skis on the enclosed back porch and can ski right out the door. Public skiing on the trails continues and groups may use a warming house, have a fire and sip hot cider. Trails are not hyped as "beginner, intermediate or expert," Donna said, because "they're all so pretty that, if they're too hard, you should take your skis off and walk them."

Rooms and Rates: Two - Both upstairs, both share bath. Rose room has double bed, blue hardwood floor, photos of the four seasons on the farm. Blue room has maple bed of Don's mother. Both have Laura Ashley quilts, country decor. $30 single, $35 double. Add tax.

Meals: Breakfast is served in the dining room or on the front or back porches. Since guests can watch milking and feeding 6:30-8, many arrange a time for breakfast after that. It includes home-baked "monkey bread," coffee cake, muffins, pancakes or waffles and fresh seasonal fruit.

Dates open: Year 'round   **Smoking:** No

Children: Talk with innkeepers ahead of time   **Pets:** No

Nearby: 20K for x-c skiing on four trails on property, two large hills for snow tubing with tube rental, 210 acres of woods and open fields for snowshoeing, hiking, mountain biking, and picnicking by guests. Elroy-Sparta Bike Trail, 7 miles. Kickapoo River canoeing, less than 30 miles. Several Amish farms (selling maple syrup, quilts, furniture), a half hour away.

Location/Directions: Four miles south of Sparta. From intersection of I-90 and Highway 27, 1.5 miles southwest on County Road J. Chicago, 5 hours. Madison, 2 hours. Milwaukee, 3.5 hours. Twin Cities, 3.5 hours.

Deposit: Half of room rate

Payment: Cash, personal or traveler's checks only

Norwalk

Lonesome Jake's Devil's Hole Ranch B&B

Route 1, Box 104
Norwalk, WI 54648
608-637-2640
608-823-7585

Owners:
    Jake and Kitty Menn
Operator:
    Paula Menn, daughter-in-law

When Paula Menn's three children go to their grandparents', they go over the river and through the wood, but the rest of the story is quite different than for most American children. Grandma is known as "Mama Kitty" and Grandpa is a cattle rancher.

The Menn family homesteaded this scenic valley in the 1850s. The Devil's Hole Ranch was named more than 130 years ago by Jake's great-grandmother, a pioneer woman.

Creative bedtime stories about Lonesome Jake, the lone cowboy, and Pretty Kitty, the woman he loved and protected, were told to the four Menn children while they were growing up in California, where Jake was a chemist. After retirement, he returned to the ranch and the house in which he was born, and "retired" to the operation of a working ranch, complete with hired hands and round-ups.

The ranch is 2,000 acres, over which cattle roam, and it has dairy cows, as well. Visitors can watch a round-up on three weekends a year and may be shown the property by Jake. He takes visitors to his Amish neighbor's furniture and leathergoods shops and for a tour on top of the ridge.

Paula Menn, who lives in Viroqua, conceived the idea of the B&B on her in-laws ranch, redecorated the farmhouse in country decor and comes out with her children to run the B&B on weekends. She may help guests pick apples in the private orchard, then make cider, or teach jam and jelly-making from local strawberries.

A grill and picnic table are located near the house so guests can cook dinner and they can use space in the refrigerator. Guests also can use a living room and porch, the game room, on the first floor. Teas, coffee, lemonade or cocoa are served in the evening.

Rooms and Rates: Three - All upstairs, all with hardwood floors and all share bath with tub only. Downstairs there is a bath with shower. Ben's Room is done in greens with an Amish quilt wallhanging, has four-poster double bed - $35. Tony's Room has antique Eastlake double bed and furniture in walnut, done in rose and cream - $40. Jake's Room, the room in which he was born, has twin beds and is done in blues - $40. Rates are doubles; singles $10 less. Add tax.

Meals: Breakfast is served at time arranged with guests and it may include French toast or sausage souffle, home-baked muffins, Amish maple syrup, apple slices and cheese. If Jake is cooking, it may be Spanish Southwest-style fare. Special diets can be accommodated.

Dates open: Weekends year 'round; weekdays with advance reservations

Smoking: No   **Pets:** No   **Children:** Yes

Nearby: Biking, hiking, photography and morel mushroom hunts on the ranch. Several Amish farms (closest ones sell furniture and leathergoods), 2 miles. Elroy-Sparta Bike Trail, 3 miles. Wildcat Mountain State Park (x-c skiing and camping), 6 miles. Kickapoo River canoe rental, 6 miles.

Location/Directions: Located on east side of County Road T between Ontario and Norwalk. Detailed directions and map sent. Chicago, 5 hours. Madison, 2 hours. Milwaukee, 3.5 hours. Twin Cities, 3.5 hours.

Deposit: First night's lodging

Payment: Cash, personal or traveler's checks only

Ontario

Downings' Bed 'N Breakfast

Highway 33
Ontario, WI 54651
608-337-4352

Owners/Operators:
Janeen and Bob Downing

Charlie Lord was a man who took risks. In the early 1900s, he had several plots in the Ontario area where he grew ginseng, a difficult-to-grow but very valuable root that some Asians believe is an aphrodisiac and is being grown again today by some adventurous Wisconsin farmers. Lord at first had a good deal of success growing ginseng and shipping it to the markets in the Far East.

So, in 1908, he contracted with the Sullivan Brothers, local carpenters, to build a massive house on the banks of the Kickapoo River, land on which he dried the ginseng. Lord heard the railroad was coming through Ontario and took another risk: he wanted to build a local hotel for weary railroad passengers. The hotel, completed two years later, had a great front lawn and the river ran through the back of the property. Huge pillars, filled with horsehair, were shipped from Tennessee.

But this risk didn't pay off. The railroad never came through, so Charlie, Mary, his wife, and daughter Vivian were alone in the big house. He also lost much of his wealth when the ginseng contracted crop rot. Still, he hung onto the would-be hotel, working as a photographer and going into shrub sales. Vivian was courted under the giant maple tree in the yard by the hired man, and lots of ladies came to take piano lessons in the parlor.

The Downing family is the third owner, and it turns out the Sullivan Brothers' builders were Bob's great-grandfather and great uncle. "We purchased it in December 1984 with the idea of a B&B as a hobby and a service for the town," Janeen said. Previous owners had rented the house as a duplex, and restoration and remodeling were necessary. The B&B opened in October 1985.

Bob operates a trucking business and Janeen is a bank assistant trust officer, so the B&B is open weekends only, unless special arrangements are made. Guests have use of the grounds, two porches and the reading room downstairs.

Rooms and Rates: Three - All upstairs, all share bath, all have one double bed, suite also has extra twin bed. Blue Bonnet Suite has double brass bed, twin bed and sink - $30 one bed, $35 both beds. Shady Rest has four-poster, mahogany bed; Scarlett's Room is done in reds and has balcony, giving the feeling of Tara - both rooms $25 single, $30 double. Bathroom has original fixtures in bath, no shower. Rarely are more than two rooms rented at once unless rented by one party or family. Rates include tax.

Meals: Continental breakfast served in the side room or on the porch in the summer 8-10 or by special arrangement, with yogurt, cheeses, fresh fruit, cereal and two or three homebaked items such as apple bread, kolaches and cranberry coffee cake.

Dates open: Weekends year 'round; weekdays with advance reservations

Smoking: On porch or reading room only

Children: Yes (daughter will babysit)   **Pets:** No

Nearby: Kickapoo River canoe rental, 1 block. Wildcat Mountain State Park (hiking, x-c skiing, camping), 2.5 miles. Several Amish farms (selling maple syrup, quilts, furniture) along Highway 33 west and and north to Wilton. Elroy-Sparta Bike Trail, 9 miles to Kendall. Ornamental church on St. Mary's Ridge, 5 miles. Pony pulls and country fest, Rockton, 6 miles. Antiquing, 20-mile surrounding area.

Location/Directions: On state Highway 33 in Ontario, first house on east side of bridge. Chicago, 5 hours. Madison, 2 hours. Milwaukee, 3.5 hours. Twin Cities, 4 hours.

Deposit: $10 per room per night

Payment: Cash, personal or traveler's checks only

Kendall

Dusk to Dawn B&B

Route 1, Box 191
Kendall, WI 54638
608-463-7547

Owners/Operators:
Gail and Fritz Miller

This B&B gets some guests who are visiting relatives in the area, or attending a wedding, or have business with area companies. But most guests come for one business only: biking (as in bicycle, not motorcycle).

Kendall is the headquarters for the Elroy-Sparta Bike Trail, a national treasure. Built in 1964 on 32 miles of former Chicago-Northwestern Railroad bed, the trail is attracting more bikers every year as the word is spread. The trail is of finely ground limestone and has only a 3 percent grade, a real treat in the steep hills and valleys carved by rivers and streams. Bicyclists pass through three tunnels, one three-quarters of a mile long, while on the trail (snowmobilers use it in the winter, though the tunnels are closed to prevent frost damage).

Fritz Miller is one of the directors of the bike trail board. "We'd been talking at meetings about the need for accommodations or a B&B," he said, since Kendall and some of the other small towns on the trail have no motels or hotels. "We're used to working with people," said Gail, having raised nine children on a farm and run a supper club for 15 years.

Millers bought the house on Medbury Street in 1986 and opened the B&B in August. The former owners had done major renovation to walls, ceiling and woodwork. The home was built in 1906 and the land owned by by both the man named Kendall and the man for whom Medbury Street was named. International Harvester also owned it. The Berg family held it the longest, from 1910-1954.

Millers came to this village after a daughter and son-in-law took over the family farm. They wallpapered, painted, added a tub and shower, and returned two small rooms to the original one-room state.

Rooms and Rates: Four - All upstairs, all share bath with tub and shower. Some modern decor. Large room with two double iron beds and crib - $40. Large room with two double beds, red rose carpeting - $40. Room with king waterbed, antiques - $35. Small room in green, double bed - $30. Rates are doubles. Each additional person, $5. Add tax.

Meals: Breakfast is served buffet-style at a pre-arranged time in the dining room or on the deck outdoors. It includes fruit and juice, yogurt, dry cereal, muffins, toast and pastries.

Dates open: Year 'round   **Smoking:** Yes

Children: Yes (crib available)   **Pets:** No

Nearby: Elroy-Sparta Bike Trail, 3 blocks. (Shuttle service from points on trail available.) Fritz organizes guided nature tours of the area. Wildcat Mountain State Park (x-c skiing, camping), Ontario, 12 miles. Kickapoo River canoe rental, 12 miles. Amish farms, antiquing.

Location/Directions: Kendall is on Highway 71 southeast of Tomah. B&B is on Medbury Street, also known as County Road W; follow County Road W signs through town to north side of town, second to last house on the left. Chicago, 4.5 hours. Madison, 1.5 hours. Milwaukee, 3.5 hours. Twin Cities, 4 hours.

Deposit: First night's lodging

Payment: Cash, personal or traveler's checks only

LaFarge

Trillium

Route 2, Box 121
LaFarge, WI 54639
608-625-4492

Owner/Operator:
Rosanne Boyett

This cottage on an 85-acre farm feels like Grandma's because it *was* Grandma's. "It came from the little town of Bloomingdale and was moved here to be Grandma's house after her husband died so she could stay on the farm and live next door to the main house," said Rosanne Boyett, who, with her husband, bought this farm in 1981. They are no relation to the previous owners, but know them.

When Rosanne and Joe Swanson bought it, the buildings had been used as a summer home only and needed repair. No problem, as these two thrive on home fix-up projects. Soon the little cottage had a huge fireplace of rock Joe hauled from the west fork of the Kickapoo River.

Other touches appeared. Despite the kitchen's electric range, refrigerator and hot and cold water, anyone's grandma might still be at home here. The woodburning cookstove works. Handmade quilts and hand-stitched doilies and other linens pop up all around. The curtains have a homemade charm that doesn't come from designer "country" stores.

The concept of a cottage and breakfast service came up long ago. "We used to live on a smaller farm and the farm next door had two houses. We kept saying, 'Wouldn't it be fun to fix up that farmhouse and rent it to people who would bring their kids to stay on a farm?' " Rosanne said. Since Trillium opened in 1984, families, honeymooners and 45th wedding anniversary couples have come.

The 85 acres -- half fields of corn, hay and oats; half hilly woods with a brook and waterfall -- are free to explore. Guests can visit with a half dozen calves, a few sheep and lambs, a laying flock and broilers, a couple goats and pheasants, all of which are raised without feed that contains growth hormones and medicines. Guests can climb the treehouse, too. Rosanne's three children allow guests privacy. Deer are often seen along the long "driveway," as are owls, hawks, grouse, pheasant and rabbits. An open porch is appreciated in the summer. Upon arrival, the refrigerator is stocked, the fire is laid, and flannel sheets are on the bed.

Rooms and Rates: One guest cottage - One double bed, one double hide-a-bed in living room, bathroom, separate room with tub only. Completely furnished with kitchen. Oil or wood heat. Hammock under apple tree. $52.50 double. Each additional person, $10.50 Children 12 and under free. Add tax. Weekday rates November through April - $42. Singles $37.50 year 'round. Weekly rates.

Meals: Rosanne brings two fresh-baked breads each morning, such as popovers, pearkuchen, maple (syrup) muffins, various sourdoughs, nut breads and raisin breads, plus two kinds of homemade jams and jellies. Time is arranged with guests the night before. Special diets can be accommodated. Refrigerator has farm's eggs, Amish butter and cheese, juices, milk and lemonade. Coffee beans, grinder; teas.

Dates open: Year 'round

Smoking: Yes

Children: Yes

Pets: No

Nearby: Woods, hills and treehouse on farm. Several Amish farms (selling maple syrup, quilts, furniture) begin 1/4 mile away. Elroy-Sparta Bike Trail, 20 miles. Wildcat Mountain State Park (x-c skiing, camping) in Ontario, 13 miles. Kickapoo River canoe and innertube rentals, 8 miles. Norskadalen (skiing and nature trails), 12 miles.

Location/Directions: Located on Salem Ridge Road, across from Buckeye Ridge Road, off County Road D about 12 miles east of Westby. Detailed instructions and map sent (and are necessary). Chicago, 4.5 hours. Madison, 2.5 hours. Milwaukee, 4.5 hours. Twin Cities, 4.5 hours.

Deposit: Half of room rate

Payment: Cash, personal or traveler's checks only

Westby

Westby House

200 W. State St.
Westby, WI 54667
608-634-4112

Owners/Operators:
Patricia Smith & partners

Patricia Smith knew exactly what she wanted: to combine her interest in antiques and decorating skills with the restaurant and bookkeeping experience of her friend, daughter and son-in-law by renovating an historic home into a restaurant, shop and guest home.

Smith, Annette and Philip Park and Robert Hektner were all Minneapolis residents who took the plunge together after finding the house they wanted in Westby. It met their structural and financial specifications, as well as those for being in a small town, yet a certain distance to the Twin Cities and a college town (LaCrosse).

Between October 1984, when Smith moved to Westby from Minneapolis, to July 1985, when the Westby House opened, "20 tons of plaster were taken out," she said. While the original woodwork, lights and stained glass in this Victorian home remain, it needed rewiring, replumbing, and redecorating, new ceilings, new porch pillars and railing, as well as the addition of a commercial kitchen for the first floor restaurant. Getting the original buffet up the stairs to the second floor must have been a sight to see, and Smith vows the giant piece is never coming back down.

Built for Martin Bekkedahl, a Norwegian businessman who owned a bank and lumber business in northern Wisconsin and was the first to plant tobacco in the county, the Westby House had only one other owner since its first use in 1892. Throughout the house, antiques are for sale, as are gifts, wallpapers, lace and quilts. The second floor has space for meetings or a two-room suite in the turret room.

Rooms and Rates: Four - All upstairs. Anniversary Suite has a queen brass bed, fainting couch, private bath with tub - $54. Other rooms share a bath with tub and shower, and a half bath. The Greenbrier Room has two double white iron beds and a sink - $44. The Squire Room has two twin beds - $38. The Country Room has a queen iron bed, quilt, tin ceiling - $38. Add tax.

Meals: Continental breakfast of fruit and homemade muffins is included in the room rate. Three meals served in restaurant, open 7:30 a.m.-9 p.m. daily.

Dates open: Year 'round

Smoking: Yes

Children: Yes

Pets: No

Nearby: Located in town, just a walk to stores and churches. X-c skiing, 1.5 miles. Amish community, 5 miles. Biking, Kickapoo River canoe rental, 8 miles. LaCrosse is 29 miles to the northwest.

Location/Directions: Highways 14/61 run through town. Turn southwest on State Street, inn is on the next righthand corner. Chicago, 4.5 hours. Madison, 1.5 hours. Milwaukee, 3.5 hours. Twin Cities, 4 hours.

Deposit: 20 percent

Payment: Cash, personal or traveler's check, VISA or MasterCard

Viroqua

Serendipity Farm

Route 3, Box 162
Viroqua, WI 54665
608-637-7708

Owners/Operators:
Suzanne and Forrest Garrett

When Suzanne Garrett looks off in the distance and says, "The girls are out to play," it has nothing to do with children. She's speaking of young cows, and you can bet that every one has a name. In a tour of the farmyard and barn, it's soon clear they are all special to her: the draft horses, the dairy cows, the pigs, chickens, ducks, geese, kittens and the horse and mule in the pasture across the street.

The Garretts have farmed all of their lives, and all of their farms have had just about every farm animal possible. "I believe in being diversified. When the milk price drops, you had better have another source of income," she says as one whose farm produces 500,000 gallons of milk from her "girls" every year.

Diversification was the reason for starting a B&B in the fall of 1983, the first in this part of the state. "Nobody knew what it was. My first brochures said '*bread and breakfast*' because I didn't see a proof and the typesetter didn't know." But the former Adams family farm, more than 100 years in that family, turned out to be an all-season setting for the two rooms in the main farmhouse and the private stone cottage, more than 50 years old itself.

On hot days, guests raft or tube in the clean, sandy west fork of the Kickapoo River, which runs below the house and cottage, only about waist-deep. A porch in the house and a deck on the cottage overlook the river, in which ducks paddle along. In other seasons, as well, the 300 acres provide plenty of trails to hike, x-c ski or snowshoe. Kids can help gather eggs and pet the young cows, and some guests want to help with simple farm chores when the Garretts are not on a tight schedule (milk five minutes too late and the "girls" get udderly uppity, so to speak). On the other hand, "some people don't come near the cows" and prefer a quiet, private getaway. Either way, it's hard to ignore Sam the Dog, who practically does backflips to please the guests.

Rooms and Rates: Two upstairs in farm house, plus stone cottage. Farm house rooms - Both share bath with shower only. Blue room has two double beds done in rust tones. Rose room has queen bed, white iron twin day bed, ceiling fan. $35 single. Each additional person, $5. Cottage sleeps 8 maximum, has two divided rooms upstairs with a queen and a full bed, modern paneling and ceilings. Downstairs, living room, dining room, kitchen and bath with tub and shower. $50 single. Each additional person, $5. Add tax.

Meals: House guests - The 8:30 breakfast is often cooked on Home Comfort woodstove and served family-style on four-season porch overlooking river or in kitchen. It includes fresh brown eggs, fresh applesauce, sausage, ham and potatoes. In cottage, breakfast is serve-yourself; homemade bread is on porch each morning.

Dates open: Year 'round   **Smoking:** Yes

Children: Yes   **Pets:** No

Nearby: Woods and hills, tubing and rafting or wading in west fork of Kickapoo, x-c skiing on trails all on farm. Canoe rental, 6 miles. Several Amish farms (selling maple syrup, quilts and furniture) begin about 4 miles. Wildcat Mountain State Park (x-c skiing, camping) in Ontario, 17 miles.

Location/Directions: Located on County Road S between Route 82 and Avalanche, or 1.5 miles north of Route 82 on S. Detailed instructions and map sent. Map also provided to Amish farms in area and of trails on farm. Chicago, 4 hours. Madison, 2 hours. Milwaukee, 4 hours. Twin Cities, 4 hours.

Deposit: First night's lodging

Payment: Cash, personal or traveler's checks only

Viroqua

Viroqua Heritage Inn

220 E. Jefferson St.
Viroqua, WI 54665
608-637-3306

Owner/Operator:
Nancy Rhodes

When Nancy Rhodes was a little girl visiting her grandmother in Viroqua, she fell in love with the old Boyle mansion on Jefferson Street. There were other huge old homes on this tree-lined street, but the Boyle mansion was her favorite. There was something about the Queen Anne tower with the windows and the balcony, and the metal flower garlands in full color.

In 1986, Rhodes, formerly of California, bought the house and opened it as a B&B. Two of her guest rooms, the Heavrin and the Weber, are named after her local ancestors. And the 1840s four-poster bed in the Heavrin room was the wedding bed of Mary Ann Cox and William Heavrin, the bed in which Mary Ann gave birth to her children.

Guests have full use of the home downstairs the way Lewis and Ella Tate Boyle did after it was built for them in 1890. Two fireplaces can be used by guests, as can the antique baby grand piano or the victrola in the music room. Look closely at the brass and crystal chandeliers -- they're made for both gas and electricity. And the oak woodwork on the floor, walls and up the staircase, goes on forever.

In addition to original furnishings, such as the oak buffet in the dining room, the house has many Victorian touches -- period antiques, oriental rugs, leaded glass, beveled windows. The decorating took place after many weeks of removing linoleum and carpet from floors, replastering walls that crumbled when the old wallpaper was removed, and stripping and sanding woodwork.

Fresh flowers and greeting cards are placed in rooms. Weddings, receptions, and meetings can be accommodated, and mystery weekends are available.

Rooms and Rates: Four - All on second floor, named after families, with double beds, sharing bath with clawfoot tub, no shower (half bath available off dining room; plans call for more baths to be installed). Heavrin Room is dark green turret room with 1840s four-poster bed, turret seat - $50. Weber Room has bay window, two double antique beds, done in pink, blue and white - $60. Boyle Room has birdseye maple woodwork and dresser, done in pinks - $47. Olson Room is the smallest room (once the servant's quarters), done in white and blue - $40. All rates singles or doubles. Each additional person, $5. Add tax.

Meals: Breakfast is served in the dining room, upstairs balcony or in rooms by special arrangement, at guests' convenience. It includes an entree, muffins and bread, fresh ground coffee, fresh fruit, juices and homemade jam. Many of the breakfast ingredients may have been grown in the garden.

Dates open: Year 'round   **Smoking:** Porch and balcony only

Children: Yes   **Pets:** No

Nearby: Wildcat Mountain State Park (x-c skiing, camping), 25 miles. Norskedalen (x-c skiing, nature trails, restored buildings), 20 miles. Mississippi River fishing, 19 miles. Several Amish farms (selling maple syrup, quilts, furniture) begin in 12 miles. Meals at farm homes, 8 miles. Local museum, golf.

Location/Directions: Jefferson is a main street at one of two traffic lights; house is two blocks east of the light. Chicago, 4.5 hours. Madison, 1.5 hours. Milwaukee, 3.5 hours. Twin Cities, 4 hours.

Deposit: Half of room rate

Payment: Cash, personal or traveler's checks, VISA, MasterCard or AMEX

Mineral Point

The Chesterfield Inn
20 Commerce St.
Mineral Point, WI 53565
608-987-3682

Owner: V. Duane Rath
Managers:
Laura and Kerry Doll

As Mineral Point's lead mines prospered, business came and went via stagecoach. In about 1834, this two-story building, built in the stone Cornish style prominent in the heavily Cornish area, became a downtown stagecoach stop.

But even before the building, miners desperate for work, regardless of living conditions, carved themselves "badger holes" in the limestone cliffs near the mines. These tiny caves served as dwellings until these hardy men could afford housing. In back of the Chesterfield Inn is one of a few badger holes remaining, where guests can see an opening for a stove pipe and imagine spending a cold, cramped winter.

In between the 1830s and now, lead and zinc mines came and went, but the building remains. It was later owned by a foundry once located across the street. Eventually it became part of a lumberyard and the front of the building was removed so the first floor could be used as a garage. By 1986, it had weathered a series of owners.

Enter V. Duane Rath, owner of Rath Manufacturing Co. in Janesville, which makes stainless steel tubing. Rath had been coming to Mineral Point on weekends for about 15 years and had done historical renovation in Janesville. Enjoying those projects, Rath decided to return the building to its original purpose: accommodation of travelers.

The inn and restaurant opened June 17, 1986, after major renovation by more than a dozen workers, taking 17 hectic days. The first-floor restaurant serves three meals a day, including soups, salads, homebaked breads, pasta and meat entrees, and, of course, the Cornish pasty. Guest rooms are upstairs. In summer, all meals are served on a patio that has been added between the house and the limestone cliff.

Guests find an amenities basket in the room with French soaps, shampoo and a sampler of Rosebeary Candies, hand-dipped chocolates made in town.

Rath also owns and operates a new four-guestroom inn on Shake Rag Alley in Mineral Point, for which reservations can be made through the Chesterfield Inn.

Rooms and Rates: Four - All upstairs, double beds, antique-furnished, sharing two restrooms and shower room. Mini-suite with sitting room, mahogany bedroom set and rose tones - $50. Other three rooms - $40. Room 2, matching cottage bedroom set from Maine. Room 3, carved oak headboard. Prices are for singles or doubles. Additional person on rollaway cot, $10. Add tax.

Meals: Continental breakfast is served in the first-floor dining room 7-11 and includes homebaked croissant or muffin. Full breakfast, lunch and dinner available in restaurant or outdoors on patio daily. Small ice cream parlor serves homemade waffle cones.

Dates open: May through October

Smoking: Yes

Children: Yes

Pets: No

Nearby: Pendarvis Cornish restoration, 5 blocks. Downtown, 1 block. House on the Rock, 17 miles. American Players Theater (Shakespeare and Chekhov professional theater under the stars) in Spring Green, 22 miles. Frank Lloyd Wright buildings, 20 miles. Artists and craftspeople.

Location/Directions: From 151, follow signs to downtown, turn right at bottom of the hill 1 block. Parking across street. Chicago, 3 hours. Madison, 1 hour. Milwaukee, 2.5 hours. Twin Cities, 5.5 hours.

Deposit: Full amount

Payment: Cash, personal or traveler's checks, VISA or MasterCard

Mineral Point

The Duke House

618 Maiden St.
Mineral Point, WI 53565
608-987-2821

Owners/Operators:
Darlene and Tom Duke

Some people need more persuading than others to take the plunge and get into the B&B business. It took a bout of nearly fatal meningitis for Tom and Darlene Duke to open theirs. Tom, an insurance adjuster in central Illinois, "was fine in the morning and in a coma in the afternoon," said Darlene. "He was lucky to recover with no ill affects. We said, 'Life's too short. We should do something we could do together and enjoy.' " They looked at antique shops and tea rooms and then saw a TV segment on B&Bs. "We looked at each other and said, 'We could do that,' " she said. But they agreed a viable business needed to be located elsewhere.

They decided on Mineral Point, captivated by the area's hills and valleys, fall colors and historic appreciation. After nine months of looking for a house, they were about to rent an apartment when the rental agent had his home up for sale. A few months later, in July 1983, the Duke House opened.

The house was built prior to the turn of the century. For a time, long before school buses, it served as a rooming house for high school girls who lived in the country but stayed in town going to school during the week. (They brought food from home and heated it up on hot plates.) A banker and his wife also owned it, doing major renovation such as taking out walls and adding a fireplace.

All in all, it was in good shape. "Underneath the paint and wallpaper we've put on, there's only one layer of paint and wallpaper. For a turn-of-the-century house, that's extraordinary," Darlene said.

A social hour for guests is from 6-7 p.m., with tea and wine. Tom and Darlene add a "just folks" atmosphere to a finely furnished home: "We don't want anybody to think they have to dress up for the social hour." Birds are feeding at the window during breakfast. The wildflower garden and backyard are open to guests, and fresh flowers are placed in bedrooms.

Rooms and Rates: Three - All upstairs with hardwood floors, oriental rugs, tie-back curtains, air-conditioned, screened windows, and Colonial furnishings, including two reading chairs. All share large bathroom with tub and shower. Largest room has queen pencil-post Sheraton bed and sitting area. Second room has queen bed with crocheted canopy. Third room has double brass bed. $37 single, $47 double. Add tax.

Meals: Breakfast is served in the dining room 7-9 and includes assorted homemade baked goods (muffins, scones, tea biscuits, coffeecakes), farm fresh eggs, toast, and a juice drink ("the Duke House version of Orange Julius"). Special diets can be accommodated. Coffee and tea provided on tea tray outside the guest rooms at 7 a.m.

Dates open: Year 'round

Smoking: No

Children: No

Pets: No

Nearby: Pendarvis Cornish restoration, 1 mile. Downtown, 5 blocks. House on the Rock, 17 miles. American Players Theater (Shakespeare and Chekhov professional theater under the stars) in Spring Green, 22 miles. Frank Lloyd Wright buildings, 20 miles. Artists and craftspeople.

Location/Directions: Located on southwest corner of Highway 151 and Maiden Street, blue house with white trim. Chicago, 3 hours. Madison, 1 hour. Milwaukee, 2.5 hours. Twin Cities, 5.5 hours.

Deposit: One night's lodging

Payment: Cash, personal or traveler's checks only

Mineral Point

The Jones House

215 Ridge St. (Hwy. 151)
P.O. Box 130
Mineral Point, WI 53565
608-987-2337

Owners: June and Art Openshaw and family
Innkeeper: Tom Openshaw, son

    This 1906 red brick home has been owned by only two families -- the original builders and the Openshaws. William A. Jones, a Welshman who came to the Mineral Point area in 1851, had the house built after he served for eight years as President McKinley's Commissioner of Indian Affairs. He and his family were involved in just about any kind of business going on in Mineral Point -- stockholders in the Mineral Point Zinc Company, involvement in the bank and railroad. Jones also was superintendent of county schools.
    For more than 50 years, Jones' heirs thought they might one day return to live in the house. A housekeeper periodically came in to maintain the boarded-up house. But the last daughter died in 1986.
    The Openshaws were able to purchase the house in October 1986, as Tom was a friend of one of the family members. They discovered an unheard-of interior condition: original wallpaper still in good condition, original and ornate woodwork never painted over, fireplaces with original tiles, and curtains folded and put in drawers.
    The Bartlett, Ill., couple first thought about doing a B&B in New England, but decided to stay closer to home. "We are going to retire in a couple of years, and we want to spend more time here," said June Openshaw of herself and husband Art. Son Tom lives on the third floor and runs the B&B, which opened in June.
    The place is clearly of mansion proportions. There are seven fireplaces, three of which can be seen standing in the lobby. A 12-foot, curved window seat is made of maple. The music room has a handpainted ceiling and original light fixtures and bulbs. A handpainted mural on canvas walls is in the dining room, with a split mahogany buffet. The round balcony on the second floor highlights a skylight and chimney. Guests have use of the living rooms on the first floor.

Rooms and Rates: Four - All on second floor with fireplaces; baths have clawfoot tubs only, shower available on third floor. One suite has sitting room, private bath - $65. One room has private bath and original fixtures - $60. Second suite has green fireplace, sink in sitting room - $55. Second room has blue Delft tile from Netherlands on fireplace - $45. $55 and $45 rooms share bath. Prices are doubles or singles. Each additional person, $10. Add tax.

Meals: Breakfast served in dining room at a time arranged the night before and may include a main entree, homemade muffins and fresh fruit.

Dates open: Year 'round   **Smoking:** Not at breakfast table

Children: Young children not recommended   **Pets:** No

Nearby: Pendarvis Cornish restoration, 1 mile. Downtown, 4 blocks. House on the Rock, 17 miles. American Players Theater (Shakespeare and Chekhov professional theater under the stars) in Spring Green, 22 miles. Frank Lloyd Wright buildings, 20 miles. Artists and craftspeople.

Location/Directions: Located on the north side of Highway 151, a big, red brick mansion with white pillars. Chicago, 3 hours. Madison, 1 hour. Milwaukee, 2.5 hours. Twin Cities, 5.5 hours.

Deposit: Half of entire stay

Payment: Cash, personal or traveler's checks only

Hazel Green

The Wisconsin House Stagecoach Inn

2105 E. Main
Hazel Green, WI 53811
608-854-2233

Owners/Operators:
Betha and John Mueller

Betha and John Mueller opened their inn in 1985 after owning a B&B for three years in nearby Galena. Not that they weren't having a good time in Galena, 9 miles away. "We always wanted an original old inn and this was for sale," said Betha. The inn was built in 1846 as one of many stagecoach stops along the route to Galena, then a booming lead mining and transportation hub with 10,000 residents, bigger than Chicago at the time.

Hazel Green had mines of its own. In 1853, Jefferson Crawford, who owned several area mines, bought the inn as a private home. The millionaire often hosted his friend, young Ulysses S. Grant, who stayed when selling leather goods for his father's store in Galena. He was so close to the family that he helped with funeral arrangements for Crawford. The inn stayed in the family until 1958, when "Miss Helen," Jefferson's granddaughter, died. It even withstood an 1876 tornado.

After a few more owners and a stint as an apartment house, the inn was restored by Muellers, who added bathrooms and decorated it in country decor worthy of photolayouts in Country Living Magazine. Each room is different.

Betha and John grew up on neighboring farms in the next county, childhood sweethearts who played in a band together and raised eight children, four of them foster children. They have farmed, run a supper club and operated a state park concession, all close to home. Now they have an antique shop in Cuba City, which they do not have to manage, so they devote full-time to the inn.

Though the decor is flawless, this place is as comfortable as an old shoe. John, who's quick with a joke, says nothing is off-limits in the house, including the kitchen. But their meals, served at the 16-foot dining room table, easily fill up travelers. Local red and white wine produced for their label is served at dinners.

Rooms and Rates: Five - All upstairs, beds have antique quilts and rooms are done in picture-perfect country decor. Rates $35-55. Examples include: Jefferson Crawford Room has double, ruffled canopy bed, private bath with tub and shower - $55. Dr. Percival Room is done in blues, double antique bed, private bath with shower only - $50. Miss Helen's Room has two twin beds and antique toys, shares bath with clawfoot tub and shower with Grant and Indianhead Rooms - $40. Rates are double. Singles, $5 less. $5 less for second night. Add tax.

Meals: Breakfast served family-style at time arranged the night before, for guests or by reservation, including bacon, sausage or ham, eggs or pancakes, potatoes and fruit. Family-style supper served Friday and Saturday by reservation only and other times for groups; price fixed at $12.95 and one entree item, plus house wine, all recipes from country inns around the U.S. Betha and John provide entertainment.

Dates open: Year 'round

Smoking: Not in bedrooms

Children: "Well-behaved"

Pets: No

Nearby: X-c ski trail and Hazel Green walking tour. Galena, Ill. (small town with fantastic historic renovation, museum, two walking tours, antique shops), 9 miles. Platteville (Mining Museum, Rollo Jameson Museum and lead mine tour), 14 miles. Dubuque (greyhound racing, historic district, Mississippi River cruises), 13 miles. Vinegar Hill Lead Mine, 5 miles; Shullsburg Lead Mine, 15 miles.

Location/Directions: Located in southwestern corner of Wisconsin. Take Highway 11 or Highway 80 to Hazel Green, one block from City Hall at corner of County Road W and Main Street. Chicago, 3.5 hours. Madison, 1.5 hours. Milwaukee, 3 hours. Twin Cities, 6.5 hours.

Deposit: First night's lodging

Payment: Cash, personal or traveler's checks only

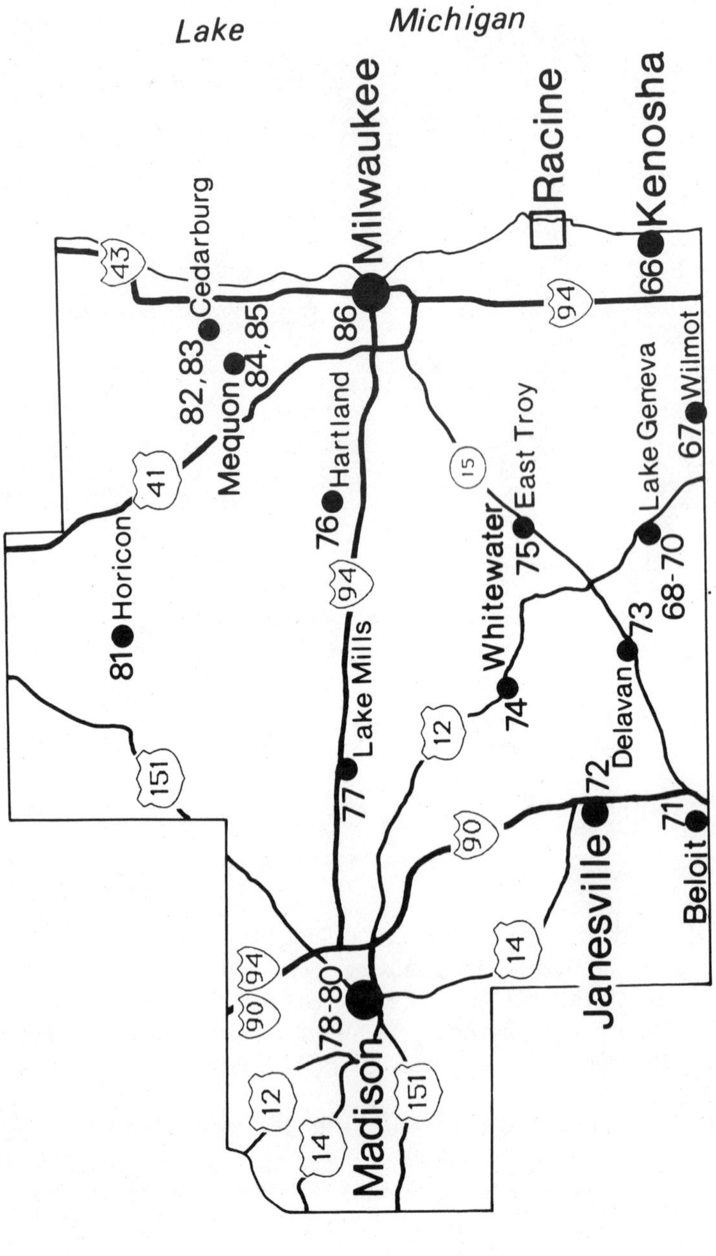
Lake Michigan
Milwaukee
Racine
Kenosha
Cedarburg
82,83
Mequon
84,85
86
66
Hartland
76
East Troy
Lake Geneva
Wilmot
67
Horicon
81
Whitewater
75
68-70
73
Delavan
74
Lake Mills
77
Janesville
72
Beloit
71
Madison
78-80
43
41
94
15
12
151
90
14

-Southern Gateway & Greater Milwaukee

66. The Manor House - Kenosha 168-169
67. Foxmoor B&B - Wilmot 170-171
68. Eleven Gables On the Lake - Lake Geneva 172-173
69. Elizabethian Inn and Kimberly House - Lake Geneva 174-175
70. The French Country Inn - Lake Geneva 176-177
71. Richardson House - Beloit 178-179
72. Jackson Street Inn - Janesville 180-181
73. Allyn House - Delavan 182-183
74. The Greene House - Whitewater 184-185
75. Greystone Farms - East Troy 186-187
76. Monches Mill House - Hartland 188-189
77. Fargo Mansion Inn - Lake Mills 190-191
78. The Collins House - Madison 192-193
79. Mansion Hill Inn - Madison 194-195
80. The Plough Inn - Madison 196-197
81. The Charly House - Horicon 198-199
82. Stagecoach Inn - Cedarburg 200-201
83. Washington House Inn - Cedarburg 202-203
84. American Country Farm - Mequon 204-205
85. Sonnenhof Inn - Mequon 206-207
86. Ogden House - Milwaukee 208-209

167

Kenosha

The Manor House
6536 Third Ave.
Kenosha, WI 53140
414-658-0014

Owner/Operator:
Dr. Clifton Peterson
Innkeeper: Mary Rzeplinski

James T. Wilson, the vice president of Nash Motor Co. (forerunner of American Motors), had the largest house in town. Built in the 1920s with a slate roof and walls 16 inches thick, this building has all the requisite rooms and appointments of mansions -- a library, ornate fireplaces, long, paneled hallways, huge rooms. In addition, Wilson had a squash court and billiard room on the lower floor. The formal garden includes a sunken lily pool, fountain and gazebo.

While the ownership and use has changed over the years, the home is still the largest house in Kenosha and most definitely a mansion. Listed on the National Register of Historic Places, the home was willed to the Kemper Center, a private Episcopal girls' school. It was the headmasters' quarters and housed some classes.

The school closed in a few years, however, and the furnishings were sold at auction. Kenosha County was turning the Kemper grounds into a park and art gallery, and the house was put on the market. With not much call for hard-to-maintain mansions, it idled there until Dr. Clifton Peterson, an orthopedic surgeon, purchased it in 1976. He traveled extensively to furnish it, saved original woodwork and put in air conditioning.

Because of his hospital affiliation, the home became used for fund-raising parties. Then requests came to rent the garden or house for weddings and receptions, meetings and conferences. The grounds are carefully maintained. The squash court and billiards room have become a meeting room. In 1986, four rooms opened as a B&B. Guests may use the Steinway grand piano in the living room, the TV in the library, the dining room and the grounds. A sitting room at the top of the stairs has a lake view.

Rooms and Rates: Four - All upstairs with private baths. Green room has two twin beds, garden view, shower only - $80. Yellow room has king bed, done in antiques with a rare prairie cradle, tub and shower - $100. Rose room has hardwood floors, overlooks rose garden, four-poster bed, glass shower only - $110. Wilson's master bedroom, done in purple, has four-poster bed with nurse's bed at foot from Crimean War, tub and separate shower stall, dressing room - $110. Rates are doubles; $5 less for singles. Add tax. Weekly rates and discounts for extended stays or multiple bookings.

Meals: Continental breakfast is served in the formal dining room or outside near the gardens 8:30-10 and includes fresh muffins and coffeecake, fresh fruit, and eggs by request.

Dates open: Year 'round

Smoking: Not in guest rooms

Children: Check with innkeeper

Pets: No

Nearby: Kemper Center (11-acre historical and recreational park on Lake Michigan shore with tennis courts, art gallery, free tours of historic buildings, fishing pier with handicapped access), across the street. Golf courses, 2-4 miles. X-c skiing near University of Wisconsin-Parkside, 4 miles. Indoor ice rink, 5 miles. Three downhill ski areas within 30 miles. Summer concerts at Alpine Valley, 30 miles.

Location/Directions: From I-94, take Hwy. 158 (52nd Street) or Hwy. 50 (75th Street) east toward lake to Third Avenue. Detailed map sent. Chicago, 1 hour. Madison, 2.5 hours. Milwaukee, half-hour. Twin Cities, 7 hours.

Deposit: Half of room rate

Payment: Cash, personal or traveler's checks only

Wilmot

Foxmoor B & B

Fox River Road
Wilmot, WI 53192
414-862-6161

Owner/Operator:
Marylyn Mayer

Don't be surprised if you go home from Marylyn Mayer's farm B&B with rhubarb or a squash or a pumpkin, depending on the season. The three-quarter acre garden is often too prolific for the use of two people, Marylyn and Fred, her husband.

And don't be surprised if you're invited to join in the day's project of bread baking, jelly making, refinishing furniture or creating stained glass. "We tell guests to consider it your own home," says Mayer, which can include joining in. For families from the city, picking their own salad in the garden, petting the dog and cat or counting the cows is sometimes the biggest hit of their trip.

"But most times people just want to come and escape," she said. Part of this large farmhouse was built before the Civil War and the old barn is held together by mortise and peg -- no nails. Since the time Anton Scherf farmed it in 1875, three additions have been put on the house. The Mayers rent the barn to a dairy farmer and enjoy the country without farming themselves (though the huge garden -- and resulting canning -- sometimes seems close to it).

Guests can wander over many of the 100 acres, which was named Foxmoor in part for the nearby Fox River and in part for the moorish resemblance when the fog settles in. Marylyn, a former high school English teacher and corporate manager, opened the B&B in October 1986 after deciding to be self-employed. "We'd been to Ireland and that was my introduction to B&Bs. In fact, I never plan on traveling any other way again," she said.

Guests can use the fireplace or VCR in the family room, the refrigerator or the charcoal grill and picnic table. Some of the decor is modern. The Mayers make their own stained glass and have used some of it in the house.

Rooms and Rates: Three - Two-room suite upstairs, one room on first floor. First floor - blue room has double bed, tub and shower - $35 double, $25 single. Upstairs, suite has one room with double bed, one with two twins, tub and shower - $35 double for one room; rented as two-room suite - $55. Add tax.

Meals: Breakfast is served on the summer porch or dining room at a time arranged the night before. It may include Belgian waffles, sausage, eggs any style, seasonal fresh fruit and homemade jams.

Dates open: Year 'round

Smoking: Yes

Children: Yes

Pets: Yes

Nearby: X-c skiing on farm fields. Canoe trips on Fox River, Nippersink Creek and White River arranged for pick-up at Foxmoor. Fox River Park, picnicking, half-mile. Downhill skiing at Wilmot Mountain, 1 mile. Silver Lake County Park (swimming, picnicking, boat launch), 2.5 miles. Horseback riding, Bong Recreation Area (hiking, fishing, hunting, riding, x-c skiing) and Twin Lakes (boat rentals, fishing), 5 miles.

Location/Directions: From or near Wilmot, take County Road W, which is also known as Fox River Road. Watch for sign on west side of road. Chicago, 1.5 hours. Madison, 1.5 hours. Milwaukee, 1 hour. Twin Cities, 7 hours.

Deposit: None

Payment: Cash, personal or traveler's checks only

Lake Geneva

Eleven Gables Inn on the Lake
493 Wrigley Dr.
Lake Geneva, WI 53147
414-248-8393

Owner/Operator:
Audrey Milliette

This lakefront home was part of a summer estate built 1847-1852 for a wealthy Chicago family. It included a coach house, an ice house, a greenhouse and quarters for the staff. Ice was "farmed" from the lake during the winter and stored.

"I arrived as a bride 32 years ago and raised my family here," said Audrey Milliette, whose late husband, a Milwaukee doctor, bought the home for her. "I fell in love with Lake Geneva and the home immediately" because of interesting nooks and crannies and charm. Though it was never damaged structurally, "the decor was ugly and considerable repair and upgrading was necessary," she said. It took six months of work with a designer and carpenter before the couple moved in. In remodeling, original doors were saved and replicas were built where possible. She added an office, bathroom and sun porch. Later, the coach house, ice house and caretaker's cottage also were remodeled, and terraces and balconies were added.

Milliette says she already has put in more than two decades in the B&B business, or an early version thereof. In 1965, she opened the home to overnight guests. But in those days it was operated as a private club. With two young children at home, "I didn't take people off the street," and guests had to be a member or guest of a member. Gourmet dinners were served "until I convinced myself that it could only be a labor of love at eight cents an hour," she laughs.

Now she operates the B&B and her real estate office in the main home. The coach house has a two-room suite and a three bedroom family unit with full kitchen, sleeping deck, courtyard with grill and balcony. It is open May 15-September only, but rooms in the main house are open year 'round. All guests have waterfront privileges at the dock in front.

Rooms and Rates: Nine - All with air conditioners or ceiling fans, TV and down comforters. Three bedroom coach house, two two-bedroom suites available. Rates range $35-$275 and depend on season, room, number of guests, number of nights reserved. Highest rates are for one night weekends and holidays; lowest rates for extended stays off-season. Examples of rooms include: Rose Vanderbilt Room - fireplace, four-poster double bed, done in rose and white, private bath with tub and shower - $55-$115. Wicker Suite - kitchenette, king bed, wicker furniture and headboard, private courtyard, private bath with shower only, $45-$125. Add tax.

Meals: Breakfast is served on the porch overlooking the lake or in front of the drawing room fireplace on weekends, modified menu weekdays, 9-10, and may include turkey and cheese-stuffed croissants or crepes Lorraine, Linzer torte, cold cereal with fresh fruit, bagels and cream cheese, apple turnovers.

Dates open: Year 'round

Smoking: Yes

Children: Yes

Pets: "With approval"

Nearby: Swimming, sunbathing, canoe, kayak and raft rentals, fishing in Lake Geneva, across the street on private dock. Restaurants, beach, shops, boat rentals, 3 blocks.

Location/Directions: Two blocks from downtown Lake Geneva (follow the lakeshore on Wrigley Drive). Chicago, 1.5 hours. Madison, 1.5 hours. Milwaukee, 45 minutes. Twin Cities, 6.5 hours.

Deposit: Full amount for one night; half of room rate for more than one night stays

Payment: Cash, traveler's checks, VISA, MasterCard, AMEX or Discover

Lake Geneva

Elizabethian Inn and the Kimberly House

463 Wrigley Dr.
Lake Geneva, WI 53147
414-248-9131

Owner/Operator:
Elizabeth Farrell

At one time, two parcels of property stretching to the lake were owned by Fred Shermmer, who made leather goods. In 1894, he built a small barn and stables, in which he hammered and cut. In 1903, he built a home on the grounds.

Since then, part of the land was deeded for a street in front, the property once was sold for taxes, and Elizabeth Farrell found a home for a B&B. A corporate dietician in the Chicago and Milwaukee areas, she looked at Lake Geneva when thinking of "retiring" into innkeeping. "I love old homes and antiques. Originally I wanted a tea room and antique shop, but that's almost impossible to manage by yourself." This way, she said, she could have her B&B and antiques, too.

She opened the former Shermmer home as the Elizabethian Inn in 1984. Then, in 1986, she opened the former barn as the Kimberly House. She serves breakfast in both, which keeps her running between buildings when rooms are full.

The Elizabethian Inn is what one would expect it to be -- a very comfortable lake home. Guests are free to use the living and dining rooms downstairs, including the one that looks over the lake, where breakfast is served. The Kimberly House (named after her granddaughter) has the "old" look with country wallpaper and decor, plus interesting antiques. The 12-foot table on which Shermmer worked on harnesses has been lowered four inches and is where guests eat breakfast. The fireplace and kitchen are available for guests' use. The sitting room formerly was a box stall and one of three original stable doors is in use in the first floor. Upstairs, the hay loft has become four guest rooms with private baths.

All guests have waterfront privileges at the dock in front.

Rooms and Rates: Kimberly House: Four - All upstairs with private baths, showers only. #1 has white iron bed with canopy. #2 has two twins with a half-canopy on ceiling. #3 has antique bed with ceiling canopy. #4 is done in purples with canopy effect, hired man's bed used as couch. Elizabethian Inn: Five - Four rented at once, all upstairs. #1 and #3 share tub and shower. #1 has lake view, poster bed, private half-bath. #2 has antique lace canopy bed, bath with shower only. #3 has double and twin bed, done in yellows. #4 has French Provincial bed, done in yellows and greens, bath with tub and shower. #5 has antique bed, done in yellow and blue, bath with shower only. Double rates are $80 weekdays, $95 Friday and Saturdays. Each additional person, $5. Add tax.

Meals: Full breakfast is served 8:30-10 and may include 24-hour omelette, fresh fruit and coffee cake.

Dates open: Year 'round   **Smoking:** Prefer not

Children: Not encouraged   **Pets:** No

Nearby: Swimming, sunbathing, fishing in Lake Geneva, across the street on private dock. Restaurants, beach, shops, boat rentals, 3 blocks.

Location/Directions: Two blocks from downtown Lake Geneva (follow the lakeshore on Wrigley Drive). Chicago, 1.5 hours. Madison, 1.5 hours. Milwaukee, 45 minutes. Twin Cities, 6.5 hours.

Deposit: Confirmation by credit card

Payment: Cash, personal or traveler's checks, VISA, MasterCard or AMEX

Lake Geneva

The French Country Inn

Highway 50 West
Route 4, Box 690
Lake Geneva, WI 53147
414-245-5220

Owners/Operators:
Joseph Navilio and family
General Manager: Peter Durnin

Three miles from Lake Geneva is the smaller Como Lake, hidden from Highway 50. The first residents on the lake arrived at the turn of the century, when the train from Chicago passed the lake on the way to Williams Bay on the large, neighboring lake.

Part of this inn arrived at about the same time. The entire guest house and part of the main inn were built in Denmark in the 1880s. Carried by ship and train to Chicago, they were the Danish Pavilion for the 1893 Colombian Exposition. After the fair, the inn was purchased and moved to Como Lake.

At its present site, the inn became well known as a restaurant and hotel. During Prohibition, its secluded location helped it operate as a casino and speakeasy. The inn and restaurant continued to operate on the lakeshore over the years, but fires in 1983 and 1984 destroyed the kitchen and dining area and a guest building, which, at this printing, were to be rebuilt soon.

Joseph Navilio, his grown children and their spouses recently became interested in the property. From the Chicago area, they had vacationed in the area for three generations and Navilio bought a Lake Geneva home in the early 1980s.

One million dollars and months longer than originally planned, the renovation was complete. The Navilio siblings and spouses acted as architects, handymen, carpenters and interior decorators.

In the main inn, the parquet floor, discovered under old carpet, was restored. The hand-carved staircase, brought from Denmark, took 1,000 hours to strip. Where 20 rooms were in the guest house, 10 now stand. Each has French doors opening to a deck and second floor rooms have skylights.

Guests have use of the sandy beach, dock and swimming pool.

Rooms and Rates: Ten in the guest house, 1 upstairs in main inn. All with private baths, fireplaces, some with double or single whirlpools, done differently in small prints, stripes and florals. Examples include room in main inn: white iron bed, double whirlpool and shower, pedestal sink, TV, ceiling fan. Double rates are $115 Friday and Saturday (two night-minimum) in summers, $95 in winters; $95 Sunday - Thursday in summers, $75 in winters. Add tax.

Meals: Breakfast is served on a buffet table in the breakfast room 8-10:30, including eggs and fresh fruit. Restaurant serves two meals a day.

Dates open: Year 'round   **Smoking:** Yes

Children: Yes   **Pets:** No

Nearby: Swimming, sunbathing, boating, fishing in Lake Como. Swimming pool and restaurant on the premises. Lake Geneva, 3 miles.

Location/Directions: Three miles west of Lake Geneva on Highway 50 (large, lighted sign). Chicago, 1.5 hours. Madison, 1.5 hours. Milwaukee, 45 minutes. Twin Cities, 6.5 hours.

Deposit: First night's lodging

Payment: Cash, personal or traveler's checks, VISA, MasterCard or AMEX

Beloit

Richardson House

829 Church St.
Beloit, WI 53511
608-365-1627

Owners/Operators:
Becky Moffett, Kevin Minter

When Robert Richardson and his wife, Bessie Clarke Perkins, first came to Beloit College, they lived for a time in an apartment house on Church Street. Eventually the popular history professor and his wife owned the house next door.

Becky Moffett and Kevin Minter also lived in the same apartment house on Church Street. And eventually they came to own the house next door -- the one Richardson built in 1907 and lived in for the rest of his life.

Richardson, one of the college's best-loved professors, was an excellent speaker and storyteller. He and his wife enjoyed their new home, designed in a New England style, but ate their meals at the Commons. Bessie died in 1936, and four years later Richardson married a Rockford College English professor, Helen Drew. The second Mrs. Richardson mothered the women students and set protocol on proper behavior and dress for co-eds and professors' wives.

Becky and Kevin promise not to tell guests how to behave or what time to be home at night. B&B travelers themselves, they "bought the iron bed before we bought the house for incentive," Becky said. When the house became theirs in October 1985, they had plenty of work ahead before opening in 1987 as a B&B.

The first floor had extensive remodeling, stripping and renovation done by the first owners after the Richardsons. The original colors were dark, and now the house is light and bright throughout. Downstairs, pictures from college archives show Richardson and the original home, complete with gaslights.

Rewiring still was needed, done by Kevin and an electrician friend. "The basement had wires draped one end to the other," he said. On the second floor, 600 pounds of ceramic tile were removed, wallpaper was stripped and water damage repaired. Becky and her mother made curtains and comforters. In addition to the living and dining rooms and back porch downstairs, guests may use a second floor sitting room with stereo, TV and working fireplace. Esther Ruth, the resident bassett hound, will say hello and then politely leave guests alone, if they prefer.

Rooms and Rates: Two - Both upstairs, sharing bath with clawfoot tub and handheld shower. Double room has white iron bed, handmade balloon valance curtains, stenciled walls, done in pinks and greens - $45. Blue room has a Civil War twin bed, done in blues and white - $35. Add tax.

Meals: Continental breakfast is served in the dining room or on a breakfast tray 8-9 or at a time arranged the night before. It may include seasonal fruit, Becky's muffins or Kevin's banana bread, fresh-squeezed orange juice. Special diets can be accommodated.

Dates open: Year 'round   **Smoking:** No

Children: Not recommended for young children   **Pets:** No

Nearby: Beloit College, across the street. Park with gazebo for picnics and concerts, end of street. Downtown, 4 blocks. Lincoln Center (archives and museum), 3.5 miles. Hanchett-Bartlett Homestead tours, 5 miles. Eight golf courses within 20 miles. Historic districts in Janesville, 12 miles, and Rockton, 5 miles.

Location/Directions: From I-90, take Exit 15 west into Beloit. Follow signs to Beloit College. Turn left on Church Street, house is on right. Chicago, 2 hours. Madison, 45 minutes. Milwaukee, 1.5 hours. Twin Cities, 6 hours.

Deposit: First night's lodging

Payment: Cash, personal or traveler's checks only

Janesville

Jackson Street Inn

210 S. Jackson St.
Janesville, WI 53545
608-754-7250

Owners/Operators:
Ilah and Bob Sessler

Ilah and Bob Sessler have opened their home, in one form or another, to the public for nearly 30 years. And they've enjoyed nearly every minute of it.

When they bought this large home in 1956, Bob was a rural mail carrier and Ilah was a teacher's aide with four kids at home. The GM plant had put on a second shift because Cadillacs and Chevrolets were much in demand. "There was a tremendous need for housing," Bob said, "so we ran a rooming house for 25 years."

The huge house was perfect for it. Construction was started in 1899 by Harriet and Thomas Jeffris. Thomas was the son of one of Janesville's first residents, and he left town for ranching and lumbering in South Dakota, but returned before his death in 1900. The Sesslers purchased the home at a time when natural woodwork was being painted over, so they saved the oak stairway, ceiling beams and built-in cabinet downstairs and natural oak woodwork in many rooms. They've also preserved the leaded glass found in nearly every room.

The Sesslers started reading about B&Bs in the mid-'70s, and they wanted to open their home to travelers. They were thinking of foreign travelers, but most guests are American B&B connoisseurs or couples looking for weekend getaways. Remodeling for a B&B began in 1981, long before most Wisconsin B&B owners began, and they opened it in 1983. They travel using B&Bs whenever they can.

Upstairs on the large landing, guests find a sitting room and a small refrigerator, plus menus and brochures from area establishments and recreation areas. They also have use of the living room downstairs, with fireplace and cable TV, and the screened porch. The large backyard is becoming quite a draw for guests; Bob has put in shuffleboard, horseshoe pits and a four-hole putting green.

Rooms and Rates: Four - All with leaded glass, beveled windows; three upstairs. Master Bedroom is on first floor, the former music parlor, done in blue and white, private bath next door with shower only - $55. Blue room has three original brass light fixtures and a plate railing, done in navy and white with window seats, private bath with clawfoot tub and shower - $55. Rose room has antique rocking chair, window seat, done in rose and white - $45. Maple room has twin maple beds, a curved wall and window, done in cream and rust - $45. Rose and Maple rooms share bath with tub and shower. Rates are doubles; singles $15 less. Child, $10. Add tax.

Meals: Breakfast is served in the dining room or on the screened porch at a time arranged the night before and may include blueberry pancakes, sausage, fresh fruit, homemade banana or lemon poppyseed bread with jam from Sesslers' apple trees and raspberry patch.

Dates open: Year 'round   **Smoking:** Yes

Children: Yes   **Pets:** No

Nearby: Downtown Janesville, 4 blocks. Old Town Janesville/Lincoln-Tallman Restorations, 7 blocks. Courthouse Park (more than 100 registered historic homes), 5 blocks. Three golf courses within 2 miles and seven more within 20 miles. Free water ski show twice a week at Rock River, half-mile. Swimming at Lions Beach, 1 mile. Rockport Park (swimming, hiking, x-c ski trails), 2 miles.

Location/Directions: From South, exit I-90 and take Highway 11; from North, exit I-90 and take Highway 26. Detailed directions and map sent. Chicago, 2 hours. Madison, 1 hour. Milwaukee, 1.5 hours. Twin Cities, 6 hours.

Deposit: First night's lodging or confirmation by credit card

Payment: Cash, personal or traveler's checks, VISA or MasterCard

Delavan

Allyn House

511 E. Walworth Ave.
P.O. Box 429
Delavan, WI 53115
414-728-9090

Owners/Operators:
Joe Johnson and
Ron Markwell

When Joe Johnson and Ron Markwell first visited the old mansion that is now Allyn House, it was a furniture store packed to the hilt with modern furniture. The floors were covered with candy-stripe carpeting, the walls and much of the woodwork covered with paint, but they could imagine the grandeur hidden underneath. It took years, though, including occasional visits, the closing of the furniture store, continued disintegration of the house and, finally, fear of demolition before the two teachers decided the structure had to be saved.

In November 1984, the house was purchased and a five-year restoration project begun. A granddaughter of the original owner, Alexander H. Allyn, in 1950 removed the Eastlake porch, balconies, tower and porte cochere, which Markwell and Johnson plan to restore by the time of this printing. The Cream City brick structure is to be trimmed in bold Victorian greens, burgundy and cream, with cedar shingles on the roof.

Inside, much of the restoration is complete. There are 23 rooms, nine Italian marble and onyx fireplaces, six original gas chandeliers, and a wealth of parquet floors and stained glass windows. Restoration has not been quick or easy. In the kitchen, for example, which hadn't been used for 15 years, the roof leaked, appliances had to be installed, and five coats of paint were removed from the wainscotting with a heat gun and nut picks.

Alexander Allyn, a dairy farmer, was also a mayor and county supervisor. He had the house built in 1885 and died there in 1913. The house was designed by Edward Townsend Mix, the prominent Milwaukee architect who also did Villa Louis in Prairie du Chien, and it is on the National Register of Historic Places.

Today, small wedding receptions are being held. B&B guests are offered complimentary wine and cheese at a social hour from 6:30-7:30 p.m.

Rooms and Rates: Four - All upstairs, with double beds, done in antiques. All sharing two baths, one with tub and shower, other with art deco shower only. Empire Room has 8-foot Empire bed, fireplace, done in black and rose floral prints - $55. Bishop's Room has stained glass windows, fireplace - $50. Eastlake Room has huge windows, fireplace - $50. Butler's Room has handcarved bed, rocker, done in brown and rose florals - $45. Rates are doubles; singles $10 less. Add tax.

Meals: Breakfast is served in the back parlor or main dining room at 8:30 (9 on Sunday) and includes homemade buttermilk biscuits, rolls, breads and muffins and homemade jam, sausage and bacon and eggs.

Dates open: Daily in summers; Thursday - Saturday from September through May

Smoking: No   **Children:** Over 12   **Pets:** No

Nearby: Downtown restaurants, 2 blocks. Fishing and boating on Lake Comus, within walking distance. Fishing, boating, sailing, swimming on Lake Delevan, horseback rid two golf courses, 1 mile. Private landing strip at nearby Lake Lawn Resort. Southern Kettle Moraine State Forest (hiking, x-c skiing, camping, picnicking, mountain biking) miles.

Location/Directions: Located on north side of Walworth Ave. (Highway 11) in Delavan. Map sent. Chicago, 1.5 hours. Madison, 1 hour. Milwaukee, 1 hour. Twin Cities, 6.5 hours.

Deposit: First night's lodging

Payment: Cash, personal or traveler's checks, VISA or MasterCard

Whitewater

The Greene House

Highways 12 and H
R.R. 2, Box 214
Whitewater, WI 53190
414-495-8771

Owners/Operators:
Lynn and Mayner Greene

When Lynn and Mayner Greene thought about opening a B&B, they found it appealing because "it combines all our hobbies," Lynn said. Indeed it does, if not inherently, then by their design.

Lynn is a caterer by trade; Mayner a music teacher. Breakfast at the Greene House has a variety of specialties chosen to offer a complete meal. A homemade treat is found on the pillow at night. Lynn is catering showers, rehearsal dinners, graduation parties and "lots of barbeques and brunches for families and friends with houses on Lake Geneva." Mayner offers music lessons at home, occasionally provides live music with friends at Sunday morning breakfasts, and has one room filled with his guitar collection (including one actually signed by Chet Atkins).

But that's not all. The garden (another hobby) is at least a half acre. The barn is an antique and gift shop (Lynn has collected antiques for years), and eventually will be available for barn dances. Some of Mayner's winetasting and marketing sales seminars probably will be offered here.

And home restoration has grown to more than just a hobby. The main farmhouse was built in 1848, with three sections added later. The Greenes have spent a good deal of time "undoing the modernizing" that three families before them have done. Since they opened in August 1985, the restoration continues and is moving toward the barn.

Though they considered opening an East Coast B&B, they chose Whitewater. Lynn grew up a mile away. "I was babysat in this house," she said. The move back from the Chicago area was welcome, and they understand why guests appreciate no phones or TV.

Rooms and Rates: Five - Four rented at once. All upstairs, share two baths and have fans or ceiling fans. Grandma's has double bed, plank floor and an old clothes collection in the closet, which is for sale and guests can try on. Moraine Room - done in greens and blues, largest room, pine log queen bed. Music Room is in blues and whites, has fireplace, double and twin bed. Maple Room has birdseye maple bedroom set, wood floor has stenciled border, antique double bed. Country Sunset room has antique hats on wall, double bed. $50 double, $40 single. Each additional person, $10. Add tax. Weekly and group rates.

Meals: Breakfast is served in the dining room at 9 or as arranged the night before. It may include potato pancakes, cheese omelettes, sausage or bacon, maple syrup, fresh fruit, or Quiche Lorraine, popovers, cheese blintzes and baked ham. (The house refrigerator is open to guests.)

Dates open: Year 'round

Smoking: Not in guest rooms

Children: "Over 5 or well-behaved"

Pets: No

Nearby: Southern Kettle Moraine State Forest (hiking, x-c skiing, camping, picnicking, mountain biking), 1 mile. Old World Wisconsin (outdoor museum of historic ethnic buildings), 5 miles. Boating, fishing, swimming, ice skating on Whitewater Lake, 5 miles. UW-Whitewater, 8 miles. Alpine Valley (music theater and downhill skiing), 8 miles. Heliport behind barn.

Location/Directions: Located on Highway 12 eight miles east of Whitewater and west of junction of Highways 12, 20 and 67. Map sent. Chicago, 2 hours. Madison, 1 hour. Milwaukee, 45 minutes. Twin Cities, 6 hours.

Deposit: $20 per night per room

Payment: Cash, personal or traveler's checks, AMEX

East Troy

Greystone Farms

770 Adam's Road
East Troy, WI 53120
414-495-8485

Owners/Operators:
Ruth and Fred Leibner

"Alane and I were painting the barn," says a smiling Ruth Leibner, referring to her daughter and gesturing out the side door. "Afterward, the darn thing looked so good, we thought we ought to do something with it!" Ruth Leibner laughs easily. Now she laughs about how the B&B got started. But it made sense, since the six children were grown, Fred still worked his tool-and-die job, and "neighbors take the hay off" of the 27 acres.

That's to say nothing of the assets of the restored turn-of-century farm home, complete with hardwood floors, family heirlooms and a woodstove in the parlor that guests are welcome to sit by. Still, she didn't know what to expect for business, sort of wondering who would come and why. Now, she's found guests simply are interested in the peace-and-quiet and good water many country dwellers take for granted.

That shouldn't be so surprising -- Ruth herself has loved the place since 1962. "We were raising six children on a 50 foot lot" in a nearby town. "When we saw this, we fell in love with it."

The farm has been traced back to 1839, when 153 acres were purchased by George Ackley from the Wisconsin territory, then under President VanBuren's administration. It's been known locally as the Adam-Ray farm from other owners, and two other families also owned it before selling to the Leibners in 1962.

Ruth runs an antique and gift shop from the house. Before opening the B&B in 1986, the family built an addition for their quarters, wallpapered all the rooms and Alane upholstered the living room set. They are starting to host weddings. A warning, though, for kids of all ages: "The tree swing has caused fights -- they're out there waiting in line!"

Rooms and Rates: Four - All upstairs, share bath with shower only, with double beds and ceiling fans. Grandma's Room has black walnut 1860s Eastlake bed, original to the house, done in greens, rose and white, twin bed also - $40. Belle's Room has double white four-poster bed, done in blue floral print - $35. Cora's Room has 1880 Eastlake oak bed, done in rose and blue, twin bed also - $35. George's Room has double bed with mallard-border wallpaper - $25. Rates are doubles; singles $5 less. Each additional adult, $10; child, $5. Add tax.

Meals: Breakfast is served in the dining room or by the stove in the parlor at a time arranged the night before. It may include scrambled eggs, sausage, pancakes, homemade bread and jams, stollen, cheeses and summer sausage, or yogurt and strawberries, homemade bran muffins, homemade bread, bacon, French toast made from homemade bread, scrambled eggs and strawberry and peach tarts.

Dates open: Year 'round   **Smoking:** Not in guest rooms   **Pets:** No

Children: "We love to have kids here" (some grandkids may be around)

Nearby: Hiking or snowshoeing, picking wild fruit and berries on 27 acres, biking and walking down country roads. Old World Wisconsin (outdoor museum of historic ethnic buildings), 4 miles. Southern Kettle Moraine State Forest (hiking, x-c skiing, camping, picnicking, mountain biking), 4 miles.

Location/Directions: Take Highway 20 west of East Troy to intersection of Adams Road and County Road J. Take Adams Road north past Little Prairie Road to the farm, located on left side of road (signs posted). Map sent. Chicago, 2 hours. Madison, 1 hour. Milwaukee, 45 minutes. Twin Cities, 6 hours.

Deposit: None

Payment: Cash, personal or traveler's checks, VISA or MasterCard

Hartland

Monches Mill House

W301 N9430 Highway E
Hartland, WI 53029
414-966-7546

Owner/Operator:
Elaine Taylor

It's hard not to hum a chorus or two of "Down By the Old Mill Stream" when on the grounds of Monches Mill House. It's on the mill pond bank of Oconomowoc River; across the road were the flour and saw mills that have since burned to the ground.

Built in 1842, this building was the home of the Swiss emigrant Henry Kuntz, the miller and an architect. Taylor bought it in 1975 as the fifth owner. The fourth left it in his will to the Wisconsin Historical Society, which rented it out. Because the Society was divesting itself of various properties and because the building had a new septic system and other improvements so it was not sufficiently original, the Society put it up for sale. Note, however, that the thick brick walls downstairs are original, and the whitewashed floors and simple decor feel as though it might be.

Taylor bought it for a family residence, but for 10 years she's had a lunch-only restaurant. "I always liked cooking and I'd taken courses in France and the U.S.," she said, so the luncheons were a natural. "A lot of people said, 'Couldn't we spend the night?' and I said, 'No, I'd have to have an innkeepers' license.' As soon as Wisconsin passed a B&B license, I jumped right in," she said.

Other than smoke alarms, the house needed little remodeling. Its three stories sit between the driveway and the millpond, back from the road. A dock stretches into the pond, and guests can fish from it or use the family canoe.

But there's quite a bit of land here and Taylor has opened more of the house and land to guests. Proficient at ping-pong? The table is set up in the barn. Tennis, anyone? There's a court on the property. And behind the garden -- from which much of the lunch servings come -- is a solar-heated house, which has a built-in whirlpool and a shower. If all that's too much activity, there's always the patio or three-season living room with windows and fireplace in which to relax.

Rooms and Rates: Four - Front Room downstairs has two twin purple canopy beds, sitting area and private balcony. Second front room downstairs has blue iron double bed, half-bath. These two rooms share bathroom. Upstairs, blue room has white wainscotting, double bed, private bath adjoining with dressing room, tub and shower. Rust and white room has private bath with tub and shower. Other shower at jacuzzi in solar house on property. $35 single, $50 double. Add tax.

Meals: Continental breakfast is served on the porch or patio in the summer (or even the dock) and in the kitchen in winter at a time arranged the night before. It may include fresh fruit, croissant and cinnamon morning bun and fresh-squeezed juice. Restaurant serves lunch Wednesdays and Fridays by reservation only.

Dates open: Year 'round   **Smoking:** Yes (owner does)

Children: Yes   **Pets:** Yes

Nearby: Pike, bass and panfish caught on the mill pond. Tennis court, whirlpool in solar house, ping-pong on premises; canoeing on the pond and river. Southern Kettle Moraine State Forest (hiking, x-c skiing, camping, picnicking, mountain biking), 2-4 miles. Pike Lake State Park (swimming, hiking, groomed x-c ski trails), 10 miles. Old World Wisconsin (living, historical museum with x-c trails), 30 miles.

Location/Directions: From I-94, take Highway 83 north to County Road VV, turn east (right) on VV. Continue to County Road E; turn north onto E and go about 3 miles to unincorporated town of Monches. Cross the mill pond; inn is first house on the right. Chicago, 2 hours. Madison, 1.5 hours. Milwaukee, 1 hour. Twin Cities, 6.5 hours.

Deposit: None

Payment: Cash, personal or traveler's checks only

Lake Mills

Fargo Mansion Inn
406 Mulberry St.
Lake Mills, WI 53551
414-648-3654

Owners:
Barry Luce and Tom Boycks
Innkeeper: Judy Adamech

Though Elijah Harvey built two stories of this house in 1881, it's been known since 1892 as the Fargo Mansion. It was then that Enoch Fargo, relative of the Wells Fargo banking family, began renovating his new home, eventually adding porches, two turrets and a third story.

The Fargo home was the social center of the community. Many balls, club meetings and dinner parties were held in the home. The house once boasted 100 windows, a walk-in freezer, a marble fountain in the dining room, and a wine cellar. The yard had large gardens and a pit where Fargo kept his pet bears, Cindy and Jack.

The Fargo family sold the mansion in 1946 to Clarence ("Pop") and Edith Wendt. Pop was a local pastor who took in foster children, and he and Edith are said to have parented approximately 80 children in this house. Today, the Pop Wendt Christmas Fund still is collected locally for needy youngsters. In 1976, the Wendts sold the home. For the next nine years, the house fell into decay. In 1982, a local historian was responsible for listing the condemned home on the National Register of Historic Places to help save it.

Then, in 1985, after the house had been boarded shut for five years, Barry Luce took a wrong turn. He was selling machine parts made in Rockford, Ill., to a customer in Lake Mills. "I called on this town for 10 years and had never been down this street. I made a wrong turn -- I was daydreaming." He looked up to see the mansion. Having renovated three historic homes with partner Tom Boycks, he knew they could handle this project. Renovation included major improvements, such as adding bathrooms with handcut Italian marble, two with whirlpool tubs. A free-floating second-story staircase has been added to create a 30-foot high foyer. The inn opened in May 1987, with weddings scheduled not far behind.

Wine and cheese is offered 6:30-7:30 p.m., served on the porch in summer.

Rooms and Rates: Five - All on second floor with private baths. Mary Rutherford Room (first wife) has twin beds and wallpapered ceiling - $65. Addie Hoyt Room has oak double bed - $55. Pop Wendt Room is in greys, has double bed - $45. Elijah Harvey Room has walnut double bed, oriental rugs and double whirlpool and shower - $85. Enoch Fargo Suite has bookcases on which guests pull a book to open the hidden bathroom door, double whirlpool, glass shower, queen bed with nine-foot headboard - $95. Add tax.

Meals: Breakfast is served in the large dining room, with beamed and sculptured ceilings, or to guestrooms 8-8:30. It may include egg, ham and cheese casserole, fruit and breads.

Dates open: Year 'round   **Smoking:** On porches only

Children: Allowed but not recommended   **Pets:** No

Nearby: Rock Lake (beaches, boat rental, fishing), 5 blocks. Glacial Drumlin Bike Trail, 1 mile. Aztalan State Park (Indian Mounds, biking, hiking, x-c skiing), 2 miles. Fireside Playhouse (dinner theater) in Port Atkinson, 15 miles.

Location/Directions: Exit I-90 and go into town on North Main Street. Turn left on Washington to Mulberry; inn is on the corner of Washington and Mulberry. Chicago, 2 hours. Madison, half-hour. Milwaukee, 1 hour. Twin Cities, 6.5 hours.

Deposit: First night's lodging

Payment: Cash, personal or traveler's checks, VISA or MasterCard

Madison

The Collins House
704 E. Gorham St.
Madison, WI 53703
608-255-4230

Owners/Operators:
Barb and Mike Pratzel

Barb and Mike Pratzel met as University students. When they married, they were still students, and took no honeymoon. Four years later, at Union Street Inn in San Francisco, they had a honeymoon and discovered B&Bs, as well.

Since then, it was in the cards that this Lake Mendota home would end up their B&B. Built in 1911 in the Old Market Place neighborhood by lumber baron William H. Collins, the house is as well remembered for its architecture as for its owner. Louis Claude and Edward Starck were well-known Madison architects who specialized in Frank Lloyd Wright's Prairie School design, and thus earned the house a place on the National Register of Historic Places. The dark brick building included the familiar Prairie School mahogany beams and oak woodwork, open spaces and simple lines, plus some leaded glass windows and a "casket rest" in the stairwell for turning the corner while moving heavy furniture or, of course, caskets.

In 1939, the house was converted to a six-unit apartment building and in the 1950s it became office space, complete with suspended ceilings and fluorescent lights. Pratzels spent about $100,000 for refurbishing. A collection of photos shows guests how the place looked as offices and gives an idea of what the present owners struggled with to make the home warm and comfortable and authentic -- right down to matching hand-stenciled wall designs.

Barb Pratzel has opened her own catering business, which should be a good indication of breakfasts to come or the success of weddings or special occasions. The Pratzels want guests to feel at home; guests have complete use of the first floor. The living room has a fireplace and guests can watch a classic video movie.

Rooms and Rates: Four - All on second or third floors with private baths with tubs and showers, telephones, handmade quilts, and window air conditioners. Claude & Starck Room has leaded glass windows with view of lake and Capitol, queen and full beds, sitting room - $75. Rosaline Peck (Madison's first innkeeper) Room has lake view, sitting room, balcony, queen bed, antique rockers in greens, browns and golds - $75. Mendota Room, only room on the third floor, has sitting area with the best lake view, green and mauve decor, queen bed - $65. Old Market Place Room looks over historic neighborhood, leaded glass windows, full bed - $55. Rates are singles or doubles. Each additional person, $15. Add tax.

Meals: Weekends - full breakfast is served in sun rooms overlooking lake 8:30-11 and may include Swedish oatmeal pancakes or roulades with homebaked breads. Weekdays - served 7-10, always homebaked breads and pastries such as cranberry streusel muffins or cinnamon rolls, seasonal fruit and cheeses.

Dates open: Year 'round

Smoking: "Not encouraged"

Children: Yes

Pets: Yes

Nearby: Located on Lake Mendota in historic district. James Madison Park with boat rentals, picnic, swimming beach, 1 block. State Capitol, 7 blocks. University of Wisconsin, 1.5 miles. Shops, restaurants, art galleries, museums, theaters 8 blocks or more. On bus line. Free parking in back.

Location/Directions: Follow signs to Capitol. Located on the isthmus between Lakes Mendota and Monona, on the shore of Mendota. East Gorham is two blocks northwest of Washington Avenue (Hwy. 151). Detailed map sent. Chicago, 3 hours. Milwaukee, 1.5 hours. Twin Cities, 5 hours.

Deposit: First night's lodging

Payment: Cash, personal or traveler's checks, VISA or MasterCard

Madison

Mansion Hill Inn
424 N. Pinckney St.
Madison, WI 53703
608-255-3999

Owners/Operators:
Randall Alexander and partners
Innkeeper: Maureen Berschens

The highest point between Lakes Mendota and Monoma has been known as Mansion Hill for years, and appropriately so. Such a price was put on socializing among the city's wealthiest here that this home and the three on the other corners were once connected by tunnels so the elements did not deter balls and teas.

Since then, the tunnel has been closed. But now, after serving as home to a Supreme Court justice, a governor's sister and other Madison elite, the home has been restored to the closest possible intent of architect Alexander McDonnell's design. It is said to resemble the second state capitol, another McDonnell design.

Randall Alexander, a Madison developer who has done other restorations, bought the property in 1984. Crews worked seven days a week for six months to open in December 1985. Some $1.6 million was spent -- $120,000 per room -- to change what recently had been student apartments into the inn, listed on the National Register of Historic Places.

Guests who walk down the back stairs can see framed snapshots of the restoration. Details are important. The stone on the entryway was recarved to match the original design. The foyer floor has 2,000 handcut pieces of inlaid marble. Some marble wall and ceiling ornamentation on the first floor had been removed and stored or built over.

A four-story spiral staircase leads to an octagonal belvedere on the roof, from which the city may be viewed. Whirlpool baths have stereophonic headphones to use while soaking. Each room has remote control cable TV, an "honor system" wet bar and computerized telephones. Valet parking is available. A conference room is located downstairs. Mansion Hill Limousine Service provides Rolls Royce limos for $40 per hour, with discounts and special packages available.

Rooms and Rates: Eleven - Ranging $100-210. All with private baths, 8 with whirlpools. Examples include: Turkish Nook, ornate wallpaper, poster bed, done in greens and golds, steam shower only - $100. James Whistler Room, silk wallpaper with peacocks, private entrance to veranda where breakfast may be served, whirlpool tub with shower - $130. Carrie Pierce Room, ornate iron bed, grapevine wallpaper, skylights, marble bath with double whirlpool separate shower - $180. Rates are doubles; singles $20 less. Add tax. Special $99 corporate program available Sunday-Thursday; 10 percent business discounts otherwise.

Meals: Continental breakfast is served in the parlor, in the guest room or on the veranda at a time arranged the night before. It includes muffins, croissants, scones or huge rolls from a popular local bakery and fresh fruit plate.

Dates open: Year 'round   **Smoking:** Yes

Children: Over 12   **Pets:** No

Nearby: Located in historic Mansion Hill District. State Capitol, 4 blocks. University of Wisconsin, half-mile. Shops, restaurants, art galleries, museums, theaters within walking distance.

Location/Directions: Follow signs to capitol; Pinckney Street runs north side; inn is on corner of Pinckney and Gilman. Chicago, 3 hours. Milwaukee, 1.5 hours. Twin Cities, 5 hours.

Deposit: First night's lodging or, if stay is four nights or more, half of room rate

Payment: Cash, personal or traveler's checks, VISA, MasterCard or AMEX

Madison

The Plough Inn

3402 Monroe St.
Madison, WI 53711
608-238-2981

Owners/Operators:
Katherine Naherny,
Roger Ganser

John Whare, a British blacksmith who sold plows from his Monroe Street establishment, spelled "plow" the old fashioned-way: "plough."

In the mid-1850s, when the house and 10 acres near Lake Wingra were purchased by Whare, he opened an inn for weary and thirsty (not necessarily in that order) stagecoach passengers. The basement tavern was soon called the "Plough Inn," partly after Whare's plow business and partly because it was said patrons "plough inn, stagger out." The second floor had a dance floor, and mention has been made in local histories of "bawdy dancing" which allegedly went on there, said Katherine Naherny.

Be assured she and her husband run a much more respectable place these days. The inn was used as a single family home, and then as an art gallery for many years before they bought it in in 1985. Popular UW-Madison art professor Roland Stebbins and Hortense, his wife, lived there for many years before his death, and Naherny says some people still know the community landmark as "the Stebbins house." Rita Wlodarczyk and Lorraine Wilke later opened an art, antique and decorating gallery and shop in the home, undertaking major modernization and renovation.

Naherny and Ganser completed work with new heating, plumbing and electrical systems, insulation and roof before opening in May 1986. They had traveled in B&Bs before, but had not intended to open one this soon. "The whole idea of a B&B was something we had talked about but planned on doing much later in our lives," she said. Opportunity, however, knocked too loudly to ignore.

Guests may use the porch for games and cards, have sherry in the afternoon, borrow a TV set and use maps of bicycle routes.

Rooms and Rates: Two - Both with private bath with tub and shower, queen brass beds with down quilts and window air conditioners. Arborview Room takes up two-thirds of the second floor, has view of Arboretum, original wood-burning fireplace in sitting area, single whirlpool and wet bar - $69. The Parkside Room, first floor, is large room with original pine floor - $49. Rates are doubles. Add tax. Extended stay and business discounts.

Meals: Continental breakfast is served in guest rooms or on the porch or patio 7:30-9:30 or by prior arrangement, and includes fresh seasonal fruit, cheeses, fresh-baked breads or pastries, fresh-squeezed juice. Special diets can be accommodated.

Dates open: Year 'round   **Smoking:** No

Children: Over 12   **Pets:** No

Nearby: University Arboretum (biking, x-c skiing), across the street. Lake Wingra (sailing, canoeing, swimming), 2 blocks. University of Wisconsin, 1 mile. Golf course with groomed x-c trails, 1 mile. Shops, restaurants, art galleries, museums, theaters about 1.5 miles. Located on a bus line.

Location/Directions: Monroe is a major thoroughfare, inn is located on corner of Monroe and Copeland. Chicago, 3 hours. Milwaukee, 1.5 hours. Twin Cities, 5 hours.

Deposit: Half of room rate

Payment: Cash, personal or traveler's checks, VISA or MasterCard

Horicon

The Charly House
111 N. Cedar St.
Horicon, WI 53032
414-485-4888
414-485-3144

Owners/Operators:
Ruth and Chuck Gill

Lots of people go to lots of places in Wisconsin to see lots of things. And there are a number of things to do and see in Horicon. But what most people go to Horicon to see is geese. Canadian geese, to be exact, in the hundreds of thousands.

The city of Horicon sits on the southern end of the 32,000-acre Horicon Marsh, a wildlife refuge that's part of the National Ice Age Reserve. Thirty miles of paved parkway loops around it, from which 200,000 migrating Canadian geese can be seen as they stop over in their spring and fall travels.

Horicon needed a B&B for humans who wanted to stop over when the geese did, according to tourism consultants, so Chuck and Ruth Gill opened the Charly House. The brick house was built in 1858 and "was always known as the H.F. Krueger estate," said Chuck. Krueger ran a general store in town. "I used to shovel their sidewalks when I was in high school," he recalled. He and Ruth in 1972 became the first owners after the Krueger family. They stripped the woodwork, carpeted, put in a new kitchen, and sold it to a baker in 1976. It was standing empty when they bought it back in June 1986, having been purchased by the John Deere company when its occupants, Deere employees, were transferred.

When Gills first owned it, they converted part of the home into a beauty shop. Today, Ruth's shop is in nearby Beaver Dam and the only business operating out of their home is the B&B. Chuck owns Chuck Gill Realty; his signs are on properties in town. Someday, they concede, they'd like to be spending more time in Arizona and Las Vegas, but they're very involved with Horicon today. Chuck, a Horicon native, will convince you there's more to Horicon than geese.

Guests may use the living room and its fireplace downstairs.

Rooms and Rates: Five - Four rented at once. Gold room is the former beauty parlor; brass queen bed in wood-paneled area, fireplace, sitting area, private entrance and bath with shower only - $60. Rustic Room is a two-room suite; one bedroom has queen bed, sitting room and another bedroom, modern decor; stairway to dining room and back door, bath with shower only - $55. Rose Room has rose floral wallpaper, two twin beds, shares bath with tub and shower with East Room - $40. East Room has brass queen bed, done in dark burgundy - $40. Rates are doubles; singles $5 less. Add tax.

Meals: Continenal breakfast is served in the dining room at a time arranged the night before and includes muffins, sweet rolls and fruit. Special diets can be accommodated.

Dates open: Year 'round   **Smoking:** Yes (owner does)

Children: Yes   **Pets:** No

Nearby: Goose-watching/photography, hiking (6 miles of trails), canoeing, x-c skiing, boating and fishing in Horicon Marsh, a 32,000-acre federal National Wildlife Refuge and State Wildlife Area where more than 200,000 Canadian geese rest during fall and spring migration (roads marked "Wild Goose Parkway" encircle marsh), half-mile. Tours of John Deere plant, Clausen Park (fishing, picnicking on Rock River), downtown, 6 blocks. Golf, 1 mile.

Location/Directions: Located one block northeast of main street (Highway 33) in downtown -- watch street signs. Chicago, 3 hours. Madison, 1 hour. Milwaukee, 1 hour. Twin Cities, 7 hours.

Deposit: None

Payment: Cash, personal or traveler's checks only

Cedarburg

Stagecoach Inn B&B

W61 N520 Washington Ave.
Cedarburg, WI 53012
414-375-0208

Owners/Operators:
Liz and Brook Brown

"First class accommodations, choice wines, liquors and cigars. Good stabling and large stock yard."

— 1850s ad for the Central House hotel

And so it was "first class" in those days, when Cedarburg was booming. The years and a number of owners, however, had taken their toll on the inn, which was condemned when Liz and Brook Brown bought it in November 1984.

Most recently a bar and boarding house, the Browns saw through all the repairs and restoration necessary to see the building's potential. Having restored four other houses, they had some idea what they were in for: cleaning the original tin ceiling took three days; stripping the staircase took two weeks.

"Our primary concern was doing authentic restoration," Liz said, noting there are no reproductions of furniture. The walls are stenciled, the plank floors are stained and have rag rugs. The few exceptions: two rooms have whirlpools, all benefit from central air conditioning, and TVs are available to guests who ask. The inn is on the National Register of Historic Places.

The Browns, both teachers, did most of the work themselves with friends. The building was jacked up. Old photos were used as models for the restoration. A local carpenter did the door frame. Original doors remain, as does the building's original layout.

Downstairs, guests check in at the low-key Stagecoach Pub, open 4-10 daily for specialty hot drinks. Board or card games are available, and a folksinger is scheduled at least once a month (no smoking even in the pub). Across the hall is Beerntsen's Candies, a branch of the Manitowoc confectionery, selling hand-dipped chocolates, fudge, nuts and other treats. In the back is Inn Books, an independent bookstore cleverly located in the former kitchen.

Rooms and Rates: Nine - All on second or third floors, with private baths with showers. Two also with whirlpools. Examples include: #1 with antique brass bed, view of old mill. #7 has two windows round on the outside, square on the inside, hired man's bed and attic-like dormers. #9 is suite with 1830s sleigh bed and king-size whirlpool in corner. $45 single, $55 double, $85 whirlpool rooms. Each additional person, $10. Add tax.

Meals: Continental breakfast is served 8-10 in the gathering room/pub or on the deck in the summer and includes assorted croissants or muffins and natural cereals.

Dates open: Year 'round   **Smoking:** No

Children: "Limited"   **Pets:** No

Nearby: Historic buildings, shopping, restaurants, movie theater, down the street. Stone Mill Winery tours, ice skating on mill pond, 3 blocks. Ozaukee Art Center, 4 blocks. Covered bridge, believed to be last in Wisconsin, 3 miles. Golf courses, Pioneer Village (restored pioneer homes, barns and other buildings), Harrington Beach State Park (x-c skiing, swimming), downhill skiing at Little Switzerland, all within 12 miles.

Location/Directions: Take exit 17 off I-43, turn left on County Road C to Highway 57, turn right; or take Highway 57 north to downtown Cedarburg, where it turns into Washington Avenue. Map sent. Chicago, 2.5 hours. Madison, 1.5 hours. Milwaukee, 20 minutes. Twin Cities, 7 hours.

Deposit: First night's lodging or credit card confirmation

Payment: Cash, personal or traveler's checks, VISA, MasterCard, AMEX or Discover

Cedarburg

Washington House Inn
W62 N573 Washington Ave.
Cedarburg, WI 53012
414-272-2740

Owners/Operators:
Sandy and Jim Pape
Innkeeper: Wendy Porterfield

"Guests without baggage will please pay in advance."
—1895 notice on Guest Register

The names on the original guest register, displayed in the lobby, are signed in a more consistent hand than those in today's register, but they are from the same places: Milwaukee, Chicago, Port Washington, Sparta, St. Paul, Elkhart, Ind.

Today's guests come with baggage, however, and they're treated to elegance that might shock the Victorians -- such as double whirlpools in all but three rooms. The Washington House was the first inn in town, built in 1846 by Conrad Horneffer, a German immigrant who made the first leather trunk in Milwaukee and later opened the first harness shop in Cedarburg. His building was replaced by a bit fancier Cream City brick building in 1886.

Sandy and Jim Pape have gone even further. Jim, a former accountant, developed the Cedar Creek Settlement winery and shopping complex in the historic woolen mill. They began looking at the hotel, which had been offices and apartments since the 1920s, and they traveled in B&Bs and inns for research.

The Papes bought it in 1983. Jim worked as general contractor and had the cut fingers from installing a tin ceiling to prove it. Only the first floor's hardwood floor, found under layers of floor coverings, was salvageable. The original layout was maintained, but rooms were enlarged, bathrooms installed, an elevator put in, and everything completely redecorated in Victorian and country print wallpapers and antiques. Local residents made quilts and rag rugs. Since it opened in 1984, five rooms have been added. Part of the "country addition," they have rough-hewn beam ceilings, exposed stone walls and plank floors -- plus the whirlpools, of course.

Listed on the National Register of Historic Places, the inn is part of a National Historic District of some 59 buildings, all on a walking tour. Guests find wine and cheese in the gathering room, with tin ceiling and lace curtains, from 5-6 p.m. A sauna is located in the basement level with dressing rooms and showers.

Meals: Continental breakfast is served buffet-style in the gathering room 7-10 and includes fresh fruit, cold cereal, fresh-squeezed juice, homemade muffins, cakes and breads baked from local turn-of-the-century recipes.

Rooms and Rates: 20 - All with antiques, down comforters, phones, color TV with cable and HBO, individual thermostats, private baths; 17 with whirlpools. Some handicapped accessible and elevator available. Rates $49-99. Examples: #208, white iron queen bed, tub and shower - $49. #303, queen bed, stained glass windows, double sunken whirlpool - $89. #305 has king canopy bed, double whirlpool in bedroom - $99. Each additional person, $10. Add tax.

Dates open: Year 'round

Children: Yes

Smoking: Yes

Pets: No

Nearby: Historic buildings, shopping, restaurants, movie theater, down the street. Stone Mill Winery tours, ice skating on mill pond, 3 blocks. Ozaukee Art Center, 4 blocks. Covered bridge, believed to be last in Wisconsin, 3 miles. Golf, Pioneer Village, Harrington Beach State Park, Little Switzerland.

Location/Directions: In downtown Cedarburg, inn is near intersection of Bridge Street and Washington Avenue. Detailed map sent. Chicago, 2.5 hours. Madison, 1.5 hours. Milwaukee, 20 minutes. Twin Cities, 7 hours.

Deposit: First night's lodging or confirmation by credit card

Payment: Cash, personal or traveler's checks, VISA, MasterCard, AMEX, Discover or Diners Club

Mequon

American Country Farm

12112 N. Wauwatosa Rd.
Mequon, WI 53092
414-242-0194

Owners/Operators:
Donna and Peter Steffen

In 1844, the Jahn family used to smoke pigs in this hand-built stone smokehouse on their farm.

Today, there's neither hide nor hair of the rotund beasts. The former smokehouse is now a country guest cottage, and Easter dinner is probably the closest many of those now inhabiting the edifice have ever come to smoked ham or its hooved origins.

The farm's third owners, Betty and Jim Wright of Milwaukee, bought it in the 1950s and restored it while raising a family. They used the barn for a dance hall. The Wrights were the owners who converted the fieldstone smokehouse to a guest cottage. They added a kitchen and bathroom on one side and made the separate building, several steps away from the main farmhouse, available to their houseguests.

Steffens bought the farm in 1985. Donna and Peter own an antique shop in nearby Cedarburg, so she furnished the place and let her children or family guests stay there. Soon the use of the guest house grew.

"Originally, we started by just having other antique dealers stay when in town for shows," she said. "The publicity changed that." With a new floor in the kitchen, new wallpaper and paint, air conditioning and antiques, the cottage was deemed suitable for the pages of Country Home Magazine. Since May 1986, it's been open to the public.

As a private cottage where breakfast is on-your-own, it's a popular place for honeymooners or other couples who want privacy. Guests can walk through orchards and 2.5 acres of wildflowers on the property.

Steffens' historic log home in Door County, called North Bay Fish Co., also is available for rent by the week when the Steffens aren't using it as their summer home.

Rooms and Rates: King-size bed or two twin beds face working fireplace, decorated with antiques in whites and beiges; TV in the corner, Dutch doors. Kitchen has juice, milk, wine in the refrigerator, fresh rolls, cereal and coffee left by Donna. Bath with shower only. Private patio and table and chairs. $55 double or single. Each additional person, $10. Add tax. Business discounts.

Meals: Breakfast is serve yourself. Donna stocks the kitchen with coffee and cold cereal, the refrigerator with juice, milk and wine, and brings over rolls before guests arrive.

Dates open: Year 'round

Smoking: Yes

Children: Yes (on rollaway cot)

Pets: "Not encouraged"

Nearby: Cedarburg (historic buildings, shopping, restaurants, movie theater, Stone Mill Winery tours, ice skating on mill pond), 4 miles. Pioneer Village (restored pioneer homes, barns and other buildings), 8 miles. Covered bridge, believed to be last in Wisconsin, 6 miles. Golf, half-mile. Downhill skiing at Little Switzerland, 10 miles.

Location/Directions: From I-43 northbound, take Exit 13 to Mequon Road, turn left (west) to Wauwatosa Road (76th Street). Turn right (north), watch for small sign. Map sent. Chicago, 2 hours. Madison, 2 hours. Milwaukee, 20 minutes. Twin Cities, 7 hours.

Deposit: First night's lodging or confirmation by credit card

Payment: Cash, personal or traveler's checks, VISA or MasterCard

Mequon

Sonnenhof Inn
13907 N. Port Washington Rd.
Meqon, WI 53092
414-375-4294

Owners/Operators:
Millie and Gene Buchel
Innkeeper: Barb Buchel Haebig

Built in 1861, this farmhouse was almost a community center, serving as a place to gather after weddings or funerals, or for parties or dances on the third floor.

John Henry Peters worked for the first landowner, then he and his brother, Albert, and their families owned the farm. Both brothers are buried 1/4 mile away in an old cemetery. Over the years, mink were raised in what is now the garage, an apple orchard thrived, and corn and animals were raised. The Peters family remained in the home for three generations, until 1970.

Today, three generations of Buchels are involved in running the B&B. The patriarch, Gene, immigrated from Liechtenstein when he was 19. In 1985, he retired from the restaurant business, selling the Ulao Inn in Grafton to his chef. Being "too used to associating with people" meant he was not about to sit around the house. He was looking for something active but less strenuous. Daughter Barb proposed a B&B, which she'd been thinking about for some time.

"I said, 'I'm interested in a B&B. Would you help us get started?' " The house, on 45 acres, had been gutted and made into a family home by the previous owners, complete with central air conditioning, and then it stood empty for a year. The Buchel family enlarged one room and redecorated the whole house, using "lots of wallpaper," Barb said; her father nods in the glassy-eyed way of a man who never wants to wallpaper again. The B&B opened in 1985. Gene and Millie live in the huge farmhouse and Barb comes in everyday from Cedarburg. Her son helps out on the lawnmower and with other chores.

Downstairs, a breakfast room looks out on the front lawn, and guests may use the living room. They are welcome to use the acreage. A walking path (or ski path) is cut to a spring-fed pond. A tennis court and patio also are available.

Rooms and Rates: Four - All upstairs with country print and floral wallpaper and sun-dried, lace-trimmed sheets. #1 has twin beds with green comforters. #2 has queen bed headboard made by local carpenter, done in blues. #3 has peach decor, bordered wallpaper, queen bed. Three rooms share large bath with tub and shower. $40 single, $55 double. Suite on third floor can sleep four. Living area, wet bar, fridge stocked with beer, pop and champagne splits for honeymooners, private bath with shower only - $85. Add tax. Business and extended stay discounts.

Meals: Continental breakfast is served by the Buchels in the breakfast room or on the patio 7-9 and includes hard rolls, croissants, cheeses, homebaked coffeecake, bread or muffins and fresh seasonal fruit.

Dates open: Year 'round

Smoking: Not in guest rooms

Children: Over 12

Pets: No

Nearby: X-c skiing and hiking on the farmland. Cedarburg (historic buildings, shopping, restaurants, movie theater, Stone Mill Winery tours, ice skating on mill pond), 4 miles. Golf, 3 miles. Pioneer Village (restored pioneer homes, barns and other buildings), 15 miles. Covered bridge, believed to be last in Wisconsin, 8 miles. River's Edge Nature Center, 12 miles. Downhill skiing at Little Switzerland, 25 miles.

Location/Directions: Take I-94 to Highway 60, then east to I-43, then south to Exit 17. At "C" Pioneer Road, turn west to Port Washington Road; turn south on it to inn. Map sent. Chicago, 2 hours. Madison, 2 hours. Milwaukee, 20 minutes. Twin Cities, 7 hours.

Deposit: First night's lodging or confirmation by credit card

Payment: Cash, personal or traveler's checks, VISA or MasterCard

Milwaukee

Ogden House
2237 North Lake Dr.
Milwaukee, WI 53202
414-272-2740

Owners/Operators:
Mary Jane and John Moss

It's fitting, somehow, that Ogden House is Milwaukee's first traditional B&B. Marion Ogden, for whom the house was built, would be proud of that.
Ogden herself had a number of "firsts" of which to be proud. A feisty 4-foot-10-inches, she was the city's first probation officer. She fought for reform of the juvenile justice system, calling on young kids in jail and helping to purchase a house so juveniles were not locked up with hardened criminals. She founded the Milwaukee Boys Club, and she was one of the first organizers of the Milwaukee County Historical Society.
Her father, G.W. Ogden, a wealthy carriage maker, built her this Federal-style home for $5,000 in 1916. He lived there until his death in 1930; she stayed another 30 years. This stately, well-kept home is part of the North Point-South Historic District, two blocks from Lake Michigan. It was designed by Armand Koch, who designed The Pfister Hotel and Gesu Church. Some interior walls are four feet thick and have blanket drawers, and most of the woodwork is rare red gum.
The Mosses knew right away it was perfect for a B&B. "This was the first house we saw on the first day of looking, which moved the schedule up a year," said John. Mary Jane and John bought it specifically for a B&B. They met selling electrical fixtures, married and now have their own electrical products business. Many vacations were spent innhopping. "We talked about retiring to the East Coast to open an inn, but we were in the market for a new house here and we thought we'd try a B&B first," says Mary Jane. They bought the house in 1985 and opened 28 days later. It was furnished in a (very hectic) month, and still has original leaded glass windows in the sunroom and glass lampshades in the hall.
Guests are free to use the library's TV and VCR, the living room and the umbrella table in the yard. The Mosses gladly offer opinions on the city's many fine restaurants and give directions. Summer guests will find fresh roses from the garden in their room.

Rooms and Rates: Two - Both upstairs, with handmade quilts, window air conditioners and private baths with tubs and showers. Master Bedroom has step stool to queen canopy bed, sitting alcove, done in rose and cream - $65. Tower Room has view of historic water tower, a four-poster tester bed, done in cream and blue - $55. No rollaway cots for additional persons. Add tax. Business discounts.

Meals: Continental breakfast is served in the dining room at 8:30 or earlier (coffee is served earlier on the sunporch) and may include homemade cinnamon nut muffins and fresh fruit, served on fine china and crystal with the morning paper.

Dates open: Year 'round

Smoking: Yes (owner does)

Children: Talk with innkeeper first

Pets: No

Nearby: St. Mary's Hospital, 1 block. Restaurants, diners, jazz coffeehouses, shops, 2 blocks. Lake Michigan (beach, lighthouse, park, marina), 2 blocks. Downtown, University of Wisconsin - Milwaukee, Summerfest (and other festivals), Circus Parade, new $100 million Milwaukee Center (downtown), 1-2 miles. Biking and foot races in the neighborhood.

Location/Directions: Take I-94 or I-43 to I-794 to Lincoln Memorial Drive exit. Turn left; go under Art Center, pass lagoon, pass first traffic light and turn left right before second onto N. Beach Drive. Go up hill and turn right on Lafayette, then left on N. Lake. Detailed map sent. Chicago, 2 hours. Madison, 1.5 hours. Twin Cities, 6.5 hours.

Deposit: $30 per room per night

Payment: Cash, personal or traveler's checks only

Contents Grouped By Location

City: Page:

Alma - Gallery House.. 58
    The Laue House 60
Appleton - The Parkside.. 108
Bayfield - Cooper Hill House.. 24
    Greunke's Inn.. 26
    Grey Oak Guest House.. 28
    Le Chateau Boutin... 30
    Old Rittenhouse Inn... 32
    Pinehurst Inn.. 34
Baraboo - The Barrister's House... 80
    House of Seven Gables.. 82
Beloit - Richardson House.. 178
Cedarburg - Stagecoach Inn... 200
    Washington House Inn... 202
Chippewa Falls - The Willson House....................................... 44
Colfax - Son-ne-Vale Farm B&B.. 46
Columbus- By the Okeag Guest House..................................... 76
Delavan - Allyn House.. 182
East Troy - Greystone Farms.. 186
Ellison Bay - The Griffin Inn... 136
    The Nelson Farm.. 138
Elton - Glacier Wilderness B&B... 70
Ephraim - The French Country Inn.. 130
    The Hillside Hotel... 132
Fish Creek - Thorp House Inn.. 124
    The Whistling Swan.. 126
    The White Gull Inn... 128
Green Lake - McConnell Inn.. 96
    Oakwood Lodge.. 98
    Strawberry Hill B&B... 100
Hartland - Monches Mill House.. 188
Hayward - The Mustard Seed... 40
Hazel Green - The Wisconsin House Stagecoach Inn.................. 164
Horicon - The Charly House... 198
Hudson - Jefferson-Day House.. 52
Janesville - Jackson Street Inn.. 180

City:	Page:
Kendall - Dusk to Dawn B&B	148
Kenosha - The Manor House	168
Kewaunee - The Gables	110
Lac du Flambeau - Chippewa Lodge B&B	66
LaFarge - Trillium	150
Lake Geneva - Eleven Gables on the Lake	172
Elizabethian Inn and the Kimberly House	174
The French Country Inn	176
Lake Mills - Fargo Mansion Inn	190
LaPointe/Madeline Island - Woods Manor B&B	36
Lewis - Seven Pines Lodge	38
Madison - The Collins House	192
Mansion Hill Inn	194
The Plough Inn	196
Marinette - Lauerman Guest House Inn	72
Mequon - American Country Farm	204
Sonnenhof Inn	206
Milwaukee - Ogden House	208
Mineral Point - The Chesterfield Inn	158
The Duke House	160
The Jones House	162
Montreal - The Inn	64
New Holstein - The Farm Homestead	104
Norwalk - Lonesome Jake's Devil's Hole Ranch	144
Ontario - Downings' B&B	146
Osceola - St. Croix River Inn	50
Plymouth - 52 Stafford, An Irish Guest House	106
Portage - Bonnie Oaks Estate	78
Prescott - The Yankee Bugler	54
Rhinelander - Cranberry Hill B&B Inn	68
Ripon - The Farmer's Daughter Inn	102
Sister Bay - The Renaissance Inn	134
Sparta - Just-N-Trails	142
Springbrook - The Stout Trout B&B	42
Stevens Point - The Victorian Swan on Water	90

City:	Page:

Stockholm - Great River Farm 56
Sturgeon Bay - The Barbican 114
    Bay Shore Inn 116
    The Inn at Cedar Crossing 118
    The Scofield House 120
    The White Lace Inn 122
Viroqua - Serendipity Farm 154
    Viroqua Heritage Inn 156
Wausau - Rosenberry Inn 92
Westby - Westby House 152
Whitewater - The Greene House 184
Wilmot - Foxmoor B&B 170
Wisconsin Dells - B&B House on River Road 84
    Historic Bennett House 86
    Sherman House 88

Contents Grouped By Name

Name: Page:

Allyn House - Delavan.. 182
American Country Farm - Mequon..204
B&B House on River Road - Wisconsin Dells................................84
The Barbican - Sturgeon Bay..114
The Barrister's House - Baraboo... 80
Bay Shore Inn - Sturgeon Bay...116
Bonnie Oaks Estate - Portage.. 78
By the Okeag Guest House - Columbus..76
The Charly House - Horicon..198
The Chesterfield Inn - Mineral Point... 158
Chippewa Lodge B&B - Lac du Flambeau................................... 66
The Collins House - Madison... 192
Cooper Hill House - Bayfield.. 24
Cranberry Hill B&B Inn - Rhinelander.. 68
Downings' B&B - Ontario.. 146
The Duke House - Mineral Point... 160
Dusk to Dawn B&B - Kendall..148
Eleven Gables on the Lake - Lake Geneva................................. 172
Elizabethian Inn and the Kimberly House - Lake Geneva...................174
Fargo Mansion Inn - Lake Mills..190
The Farm Homestead - New Holstein... 104
The Farmer's Daughter Inn - Ripon..102
52 Stafford, An Irish Guest House - Plymouth....................... 106
Foxmoor B&B - Wilmot.. 170
The French Country Inn - Lake Geneva..................................... 176
The French Country Inn - Ephraim... 130
The Gables - Kewaunee.. 110
Gallery House - Alma..58
Glacier Wilderness B&B - Elton... 70
Great River Farm - Stockholm... 56
The Greene House - Whitewater... 184
Greunke's Inn - Bayfield.. 26
Grey Oak Guest House - Bayfield..28
Greystone Farms - East Troy... 186
The Griffin Inn - Ellison Bay... 136

213

Name:	Page:
The Hillside Hotel - Ephraim	132
Historic Bennett House - Wisconsin Dells	86
House of Seven Gables - Baraboo	82
The Inn - Montreal	64
The Inn at Cedar Crossing - Sturgeon Bay	118
Jackson Street Inn - Janesville	180
Jefferson-Day House - Hudson	52
The Jones House - Mineral Point	162
Just-N-Trails - Sparta	142
The Laue House - Alma	60
Lauerman Guest House Inn - Marinette	72
Le Chateau Boutin - Bayfield	30
Lonesome Jake's Devil's Hole Ranch - Norwalk	144
The Manor House - Kenosha	168
Mansion Hill Inn - Madison	194
McConnell Inn - Green Lake	96
Monches Mill House - Hartland	188
The Mustard Seed - Hayward	40
The Nelson Farm - Ellison Bay	138
Oakwood Lodge - Green Lake	98
Ogden House - Milwaukee	208
Old Rittenhouse Inn - Bayfield	32
The Parkside - Appleton	108
Pinehurst Inn - Bayfield	34
The Plough Inn - Madison	196
The Renaissance Inn - Sister Bay	134
Richardson House - Beloit	178
Rosenberry Inn - Wausau	92
St. Croix River Inn - Osceola	50
The Scofield House - Sturgeon Bay	120
Serendipity Farm - Viroqua	154
Seven Pines Lodge - Lewis	38
Sherman House - Wisconsin Dells	88
Sonnenhof Inn - Mequon	206

Name:	Page:
Son-ne-Vale Farm B&B - Colfax	46
Stagecoach Inn - Cedarburg	200
Strawberry Hill B&B - Green Lake	100
The Stout Trout B&B - Springbrook	42
Thorp House Inn - Fish Creek	124
Trillium - LaFarge	150
The Victorian Swan on Water - Stevens Point	90
Viroqua Heritage Inn - Viroqua	156
Washington House Inn - Cedarburg	202
The Wisconsin House Stagecoach Inn - Hazel Green	164
Westby House - Westby	152
The Willson House - Chippewa Falls	44
The Whistling Swan - Fish Creek	126
The White Gull Inn - Fish Creek	128
The White Lace Inn - Sturgeon Bay	122
Woods Manor B&B - LaPointe (Madeline Island)	36
The Yankee Bugler - Prescott	54

Contents Grouped By Category*

B&B: Page:

Allyn House - Delavan	182
B&B House on River Road - Wisconsin Dells	84
The Barbican - Sturgeon Bay	114
The Barrister's House - Baraboo	80
The Charly House - Horicon	198
The Chesterfield Inn - Mineral Point	158
Chippewa Lodge B&B - Lac du Flambeau	66
Cooper Hill House - Bayfield	24
Cranberry Hill B&B Inn - Rhinelander	68
Downings' B&B - Ontario	146
The Duke House - Mineral Point	160
Dusk to Dawn B&B - Kendall	148
Eleven Gables on the Lake - Lake Geneva	172
Elizabethian Inn and the Kimberly House - Lake Geneva	174
The Farm Homestead - New Holstein	104
Foxmoor B&B - Wilmot	170
The French Country Inn - Ephraim	130
The Gables - Kewaunee	110
Gallery House - Alma	58
Glacier Wilderness B&B - Elton	70
Great River Farm - Stockholm	56
The Greene House - Whitewater	184
Grey Oak Guest House - Bayfield	28
Greystone Farms - East Troy	186
Historic Bennett House - Wisconsin Dells	86
House of Seven Gables - Baraboo	82
The Inn - Montreal	64
Jackson Street Inn - Janesville	180

*Please note that these categories are regardless of legal definition and were assigned by the author, who is fully aware that someone, somewhere is going to strongly disagree. Some decisions are arguable, so please read the full descriptions and definitions in the introduction, then decide for yourself. Briefly, B&Bs are usually four guestrooms-or-less, owner-occupied houses, and guests feel like they are staying in someone's home. Country inns usually are larger and more private with possibly more amenities, but sometimes at the expense of contact with the hosts.

B&Bs, con't.   Page:

Jefferson-Day House - Hudson.. 52
The Jones House - Mineral Point... 162
Just-N-Trails - Sparta.. 142
The Laue House - Alma.. 60
Lonesome Jake's Devil's Hole Ranch - Norwalk........................ 144
The Manor House - Kenosha... 168
McConnell Inn - Green Lake.. 96
Monches Mill House - Hartland... 188
The Mustard Seed - Hayward.. 40
The Nelson Farm - Ellison Bay... 138
Ogden House - Milwaukee.. 208
The Parkside - Appleton.. 108
Pinehurst Inn - Bayfield... 34
The Plough Inn - Madison.. 196
Richardson House - Beloit.. 178
The Scofield House - Sturgeon Bay... 120
Serendipity Farm - Viroqua... 154
Sherman House - Wisconsin Dells... 88
Sonnenhof Inn - Mequon.. 206
Son-ne-Vale Farm B&B - Colfax.. 46
Strawberry Hill B&B - Green Lake.. 100
The Stout Trout B&B - Springbrook... 42
Thorp House Inn - Fish Creek.. 124
The Victorian Swan on Water - Stevens Point........................... 90
Viroqua Heritage Inn - Viroqua... 156
Westby House - Westby... 152
The Willson House - Chippewa Falls.. 44
The Yankee Bugler - Prescott.. 54

Country Inns: Page:

Bay Shore Inn - Sturgeon Bay... 116
The Collins House - Madison... 192
Fargo Mansion Inn - Lake Mills... 190

217

Country Inns, con't.   Page:

52 Stafford, An Irish Guest House - Plymouth............................ 106
The French Country Inn - Lake Geneva............................ 176
Greunke's Inn - Bayfield............................ 26
The Griffin Inn - Ellison Bay............................ 136
The Hillside Hotel - Ephraim............................ 132
The Inn at Cedar Crossing - Sturgeon Bay............................ 118
Lauerman Guest House Inn - Marinette............................ 72
Le Chateau Boutin - Bayfield............................ 30
Mansion Hill Inn - Madison............................ 194
Oakwood Lodge - Green Lake............................ 98
Old Rittenhouse Inn - Bayfield............................ 32
The Renaissance Inn - Sister Bay............................ 134
Rosenberry Inn - Wausau............................ 92
St. Croix River Inn - Osceola............................ 50
Seven Pines Lodge - Lewis............................ 38
Stagecoach Inn - Cedarburg............................ 200
Washington House Inn - Cedarburg............................ 202
The Wisconsin House Stagecoach Inn - Hazel Green............................ 164
The Whistling Swan - Fish Creek............................ 126
The White Gull Inn - Fish Creek............................ 128
The White Lace Inn - Sturgeon Bay............................ 122
Woods Manor B&B - LaPointe (Madeline Island) 36

Private Guest Houses or private cottages also available: Page:

American Country Farm - Mequon............................ 204
Bonnie Oaks Estate - Portage............................ 78
By the Okeag Guest House - Columbus............................ 76
Eleven Gables on the Lake - Lake Geneva............................ 172
The Farmer's Daughter Inn - Ripon............................ 102
The French Country Inn - Ephraim............................ 130
The Griffin Inn - Ellison Bay............................ 136
The Hillside Hotel - Ephraim............................ 132
Serendipity Farm - Viroqua............................ 154
Seven Pines Lodge - Lewis............................ 38
Thorp House Inn - Fish Creek............................ 124
Trillium - LaFarge............................ 150
The White Gull Inn - Fish Creek............................ 128

Farms actively worked by hosts: **Page:**

The Farm Homestead - New Holstein... 104
The Farmer's Daughter Inn - Ripon... 102
Great River Farm - Stockholm.. 56
Just-N-Trails - Sparta.. 142
Lonesome Jake's Devil's Hole Ranch - Norwalk.................................. 144
Serendipity Farm - Viroqua.. 154
Trillium - LaFarge.. 150

Other farm/farmhouse stays: **Page:**

American Country Farm - Mequon.. 204
Foxmoor B&B - Wilmot.. 170
Greystone Farms - East Troy... 186
The Nelson Farm - Ellison Bay... 138
Sonnenhof Inn - Mequon.. 206
Son-ne-Vale Farm B&B - Colfax... 46
Strawberry Hill B&B - Green Lake.. 100

Travel Notes

Wisconsin and Minnesota versions of *"Room at the Inn"* Are Available by Mail

Copies of **Room at the Inn/Wisconsin** make a great gift for all travelers: couples, singles or families, vacationers or businesspeople.
Cost: $9.95 retail, plus $2.00 postage, handling and tax = $11.95

Traveling to Minnesota? Minnesota's historic B&Bs are featured in **Room at the Inn/Minnesota**, a guide to 51 historic B&Bs, hotels and country inns within a day's drive of the Twin Cities.
Cost: $7.95 retail, plus $1.80 postage, handling and tax = $9.75

Additional copies may be ordered from **Down to Earth Publications, 1426 Sheldon, St. Paul, MN 55108**. Please make checks payable to Down to Earth Publications.

Order Form

Mail to: **Down to Earth Publications**
1426 Sheldon
St. Paul, MN 55105

Please send me _____ **Room at the Inn/Wisconsin** at $11.95 each.

Please send me _____ **Room at the Inn/Minnesota** at $9.75 each.

I have enclosed $_____ for _____ book(s). Send it/them to:

Name: _____

Street: _____ Apt. No. _____

City: _____ State: _____ Zip: _____

Wisconsin and Minnesota versions of
"Room at the Inn"
Are Available by Mail

Copies of **Room at the Inn/Wisconsin** make a great gift for all travelers: couples, singles or families, vacationers or businesspeople.
Cost: $9.95 retail, plus $2.00 postage, handling and tax = $11.95

Traveling to Minnesota? Minnesota's historic B&Bs are featured in **Room at the Inn/Minnesota**, a guide to 51 historic B&Bs, hotels and country inns within a day's drive of the Twin Cities.
Cost: $7.95 retail, plus $1.80 postage, handling and tax = $9.75

Additional copies may be ordered from **Down to Earth Publications, 1426 Sheldon, St. Paul, MN 55108**. Please make checks payable to Down to Earth Publications.

Order Form

Mail to: **Down to Earth Publications**
1426 Sheldon
St. Paul, MN 55105

Please send me _____ **Room at the Inn/Wisconsin** at $11.95 each.

Please send me _____ **Room at the Inn/Minnesota** at $9.75 each.

I have enclosed $_____ for _____ book(s). Send it/them to:

Name: _____

Street: _____ Apt. No. _____

City: _____ State: _____ Zip: _____

About the author

Laura Zahn is president of Down to Earth Publications, a St. Paul, Minn., writing, publishing and public relations firm specializing in travel. Her work has appeared in many newspapers and magazines, including the Chicago Sun-Times, Dallas Morning News, Detroit News, Hartford Courant, Kansas City Star, L.A. Times, Milwaukee Journal, Mpls.-St. Paul Magazine, Minneapolis Star and Tribune and St. Paul Pioneer Press-Dispatch. This is her third book. Her first book, "Room at the Inn: Guide to Historic B&Bs, Hotels and Country Inns Close to the Twin Cities," was first published in October 1986. She is co-publisher and co-author of "Ride Guide to the Historic Alaska Railroad." Zahn has worked in public relations in Minnesota and as a reporter and editor on newspapers in Alaska and Minnesota.